THE
DIMINISHED
MIND

A Study of Planned Mediocrity in
Our Public Schools

THE
DIMINISHED
MIND

*A Study of Planned Mediocrity in
Our Public Schools*

BY

MORTIMER SMITH

HENRY REGNERY COMPANY
Chicago   1954

First Printing, October, 1954
Second Printing, January, 1955

to ...
PATRICIA
STEPHEN
OLEA
and SHAPLEIGH

CONTENTS

THE
DIMINISHED
MIND

Prologue

In an earlier book I made a layman's attempt to examine the philosophical foundations on which the structure of contemporary American public school education has been reared, and made some passing references to a few of the practical consequences which have naturally flowed from widespread, if not always conscious, acceptance of the pragmatic-instrumentalist-experimentalist position. In the five years since that book appeared my own education in education has continued. I have corresponded with hundreds of parents, teachers, administrators, and professors of education; and in trips undertaken for the express purpose, I have talked with them in their native habitats, from the eastern seaboard to the western. I have continued to read with almost mesmeric fascination and a reeling mind, vast quantities of what is euphemistically called educational literature, a body of work which, as the late Nicholas Murray Butler said, is not "nutritious as a steady diet." The result of this continuing education has served to buttress my original conviction of the inadequacy of a philosophy which insists on the centrality of "growth" in education but steadfastly refuses to answer the question, Growth towards what?

The fact that my convictions remain unchanged is hardly an excuse for writing the same book over again, and I do not propose to do so. But my continuing education has convinced me that many people want to know more about the practical consequences stemming from the sort of philosophical and pedagogical theorizing which has been dominant in public education for the last thirty years or so. Having observed these consequences on a fairly wide front, and having accumulated a bursting file of data relating to them, I have attempted to write a book that would be a sort of factual counterpart to the earlier and more theoretical volume, a book which aims to present evidence in support of the thesis that learning, in the traditional sense of disciplined knowledge, is rapidly declining in our public schools, not through fortuitous circumstances but by deliberate, and almost invariably well-intentioned, design of those responsible for setting the direction of public education.

I have not been content to describe this process of decline, any more than a doctor would be content to describe the symptoms of malnutrition; as would the doctor in the case of the anemic person, I make some suggestions, in passing, for vitamin injections for the anemic institution of the school, occasionally even suggesting what the ingredients and potency of the injections should be. I am afraid the majority of professional educators will like neither my diagnosis of the disease nor my suggestions for curing it; in any case, I have tried to be scrupulously fair and accurate in documenting my case as I go along.

Anyone who criticizes public education today ought at the outset to make his ideological position as clear as possible. This is necessary because the hierarchy which has set up the controlling doctrines of public education in this country has a tendency, as its monopoly is threatened, to lump all critics of schools together indiscriminately as reactionaries, penny-pinchers, members of pressure groups, possibly fascists, certainly cranks.

To begin my creed negatively, let me state some of the things I do not believe in. I do not believe the little red schoolhouse represents the peak of educational achievement nor do I feel that the way I was taught in the fourth grade involved pedagogical technique in its perfection. (On the other hand, I do not recall that the school I attended was a prison presided over by steely-eyed matrons equipped with birch rods, which is the picture educators present of American schools before the current enlightenment.) I do not habitually sneer at the mention of progressive education: I may feel that its philosophical foundations are built on quicksand but I also think it has made undoubted contributions in method to all education. I do not wish to revive the classical trivium for American high schools and am quite prepared to admit that physics and four years of Latin may not be the ideal curriculum for young people with I.Q.'s of ninety.

I do not belittle practical usefulness as a criterion in devising a curriculum, but a school program which teaches little beyond how to fix a fuse, drive a car, set the dinner table, and enhance your personal appearance, isn't useful enough if your aim is the development of maturity and intelligent citizenship.

I do not believe our schools are hotbeds of communism and I think critics who attack them on this score not only becloud the real issues but create a hostile atmosphere in which it is going to be very difficult to resolve our problems. On the other hand, there is an influential group of educators, the so-called reconstructionists, who advocate the use of the schools for indoctrination in behalf of a new political, economic, and social order (their own, of course), and I have felt under the necessity of examining and criticizing some of their pronouncements. In certain circles this leaves me open to the charge of being out of touch with the cultural realities of the

3

times, or in blunter terms, of being an old reactionary. I shall try to bear up cheerfully under the charge.

I don't begrudge the amount of taxes spent on schools although I do think we often get short-changed by inadequately, or foolishly, prepared teachers, and that too often a disproportionately large amount of our investment in schools goes for non- or extra-educational purposes.

I do not believe parents can run the schools, any more than I believe that colleges can be run by majority vote of the alumni. But I think citizens ought to resist current claims of professional untouchability and the implication that all educational matters not on a mechanical plane, like buildings and bond issues, are too esoteric for lay comprehension. Currently educators seem to have an urge for playing the role of the exact scientist which causes them to give *diagnostic* tests and organize educational *clinics* and workshop *laboratories*. The constant use of terms borrowed from the medical profession makes one suspect that the educator harbors a secret picture of himself clothed in white uniform, applying his stethoscope with unerring accuracy to the educational heart-beats of American youth. One such Dr. Kildare among the educators, referring to arguments carried on by "the nonprofessional part of society" about "the character of the skills and the methods of teaching them," says loftily that "in reality this is not the business of society at large, any more than the kinds of prescriptions doctors give to patients should be a matter of public discussion."[1] (In other words, the message of the educator to the parent concerned about what should be taught and how it should be taught, is this: Mind your own business.) This unfortunately is not simply a case of individual, eccentric ar-

1. J. Paul Leonard, *Developing the Secondary School Curriculum* (New York; Rinehart & Company, Inc., 1946), pp. 546–47.

rogance; the American Association of School Administrators makes precisely the same point in their claim that school board members are no more competent to pass on curriculum matters "than the patient's family can pass on the scientific details of the doctor's treatment."[2]

I don't belong to any pressure groups. (A pressure group is any group of people who stand for something we don't like while our own group is comprised of public-spirited citizens working for the common good.) In fact, the only educational group to which I belong is the Parent-Teacher Association, a fairly innocuous organization which, I regret to say, sometimes seems to think that the whole duty of man is to help organize the hot lunch program and provide uniforms for the girls' basketball team.

Ordinarily one would not feel it important to state the commonplace that one believes in the public schools, except that in the eyes of some educators anyone who is skeptical of current practices is automatically placed in the ominous category of "the enemy." In the aggregate my children have, so far, spent twenty-three years in the public schools—and both of their parents have served as school board members. But because one believes in them is no reason for building up a sort of *mystique* of the public schools, as James Bryant Conant does, in which "democratic unity" is served only by everyone attending the same schools, even when they are bad schools. Schools are a social convenience and they ought to be subject to the same tests of effectiveness and competence we apply to other social institutions.

I am aware of the fact that public schools in this country are

2. *School Boards in Action,* Twenty-Fourth Yearbook, American Association of School Administrators (Washington, D.C., 1946), p. 178.

operating under mechanical difficulties, such as shortages of classrooms and teaching personnel, that amount in some sections of the country to crisis conditions. Educators deserve the support of all of us in trying to overcome these severe handicaps but we need to ask ourselves whether the educational product would be greatly improved if by some miracle these handicaps could be wiped out overnight. While the present system remains intact, one may be skeptical of any great improvement; for one thing, better salaries won't produce good teachers until the present unhealthy conditions surrounding certification practices are radically revised. As long as good prospective teachers from the liberal arts colleges feel, in the words of Professor Isabel Stephens, that "they must qualify for public school jobs in a way that seems to them absurd," just so long will they stay away from the public schools in droves.

But to come to the positive side of things, let me state what I feel should be the function of the school. Some people seem to think it ought to be a sort of social service agency, replacing that quaint old institution, the home, where all the educative needs of youth will be met; but this would seem to me to be too indiscriminate a function, resulting in the school spreading itself so thin it can't be effective in any direction. I would grant a lot of ancillary functions, but I think the *primary* function of the school *is to transmit the intellectual and cultural heritage and knowledge of the race, and in the process to teach young people to think, and to buttress moral values.* To fulfill this function is not a small or a simple task; I am convinced that lukewarm devotion to it, or outright contempt for it, is responsible for the progressive decline in the quality of public education which we are witnessing today.

Most professional educators do not seem to believe in this

conception of the school's function, or at least they are doubtful of the ability of the majority to "take" education and feel that the discipline of exposure to the cultural heritage is a luxury for the gifted minority. Now I am aware of the fact (which educators keep announcing as a startling discovery) that our high schools are a good deal less selective than they were a generation or two ago and that the present heterogeneous population of the schools is not comprised exclusively of potential geniuses and scholars or persons with superior I.Q.'s. I readily admit that the curriculum of the high school is going to have to be revised for the average student, or the student on the shady side of average, but the revision needs to be in the direction of discovering new and better methods and techniques for reaching this group with the values of the cultural heritage. I wish this were the task at which the professional pedagogues were busying themselves but I think the evidence of this book will show that they have no faith in any such objective. The personal pronouncements of leading educators and the ukases of their professional associations pay lip service to formal knowledge and the cultural tradition, usually at the end of a many-numbered list of objectives for the schools; their *practice* shows that this has been pushed to the periphery of educational aims while they are busy devising courses in trade skills, personal grooming, smoke abatement, and social adjustment. The latter may be legitimate auxiliary and incidental concerns of the school but they cannot take the place of intellectual and moral training and the cultivation of intelligence. In the current demand for the schools to teach everything from the mysteries of sex to how to drive a car, we ought to ask what we are going to have to throw out of the curriculum to make room for these newcomers, and whether they are going to divert the schools from their primary tasks.

7

I believe there are universal values in education that are good for everyone, whether he intends to become a butcher or a banker, a minister or a motorman, a professor or a plumber. The average student should not be treated as a second-class citizen of the educational world who can be thrown a few devitalized crumbs and then shoved into a variety of nonacademic courses devoid of real content. When the schoolman of today implies that education is only for an intellectual elite and attempts to water it down, or practically eliminate it, on the assumption that most people aren't up to it—when he does this, he is dooming the vast majority to intellectual and cultural subservience. The irony of the situation is that this is done by those who often talk as if they were the only legitimate guardians of the sacred flame of democracy.

Another item in my educational credo is that we must not forget, in a time when so much emphasis is placed on group action and adjustment to the group, that education is a personal, individual experience. Its purpose is the improvement of persons and only secondarily the improvement of society. It seems to me that the early advocates of universal public education in this country—men like Horace Mann and Henry Barnard—looked on education as a means of producing the good man who in the aggregate would produce the good society. That ought to be the aim of education today, to produce the good individual who in turn will be the good citizen; but the successors of Mann and Barnard seem bent on emphasizing the sociological rather than the human side of education.

To speak of education as an individual matter brings me finally to the ultimate individual experience, religion, and its relation to the schools. Education is not only the pursuit of knowledge, it is also a seeking after goodness. In their justified distrust of the overzealousness of sectarian agencies, schoolmen are excluding religion altogether from the schools, or even worse, are setting up democracy or the community or the state as sources from which to draw moral values. The secularists do not seem to see that reverence for life, a sense of the dignity and worth of individual man, the values of democracy itself, have their sources in intuitive religious insights. Whatever the difficulties of presenting them—and there are genuine practical difficulties—these insights should not be lost to the child in public school. At the least, we can hope that every teacher might be permeating her teaching, and the atmosphere of her classroom, with a contagious devotion to moral and spiritual and ethical values. I think that just as we ought to reject one modern notion in education that there is no order of goods, or values, among subjects in the curriculum, we ought to reject another modern notion that truth is only something that "works" and that problems are not solved by reference to principles but by pragmatic testing to determine, not what is right, but what is expedient. Failure to reject this notion, in and out of classrooms, produces the moral neutrality and spiritual indifference that today infects so many aspects of American life.

It is in the light of the foregoing educational philosophy (or catalogue of prejudices, I am afraid the educator may say) that I examine what is going on in our schools today. There are brave and scattered oases that still provide real educational nourishment but what is going on generally seems to be a progressive decline in learning—and it is not something we are drifting into but is a movement led by men who are themselves anti-intellectual and contemptuous of the cultural tradition. There are prophets among us who say this decline is but part of the general vulgarization of values inevitable in a society dominated by the whims and desires of

the masses; they declare gloomily that democracy can ultimately lead only to the decay of civilization, to "rebarbariza-
tion." (This complaint has been with us for a long time. In the
1870's Gustave Flaubert, writing of a plan of the French ministry for the reform of public education in which courses in
physical training took precedence over French literature, described this circumstance as "a significant little symptom" of
the rising flood of barbarism.)[3]

I am not so sure about the inevitability of the rising flood;
it seems to me that we Americans, saturated with the inferior
as we are, respond avidly to a product of quality when it is
available to us. The first step is to recognize the inferior and
there are some signs that many Americans are doing just that
as regards education; at least many of them suspect there are
flaws in the present system although they may not always be
able to spot them. I hope this book will be of some help as a
sort of spotting service for parents and laymen.

Perhaps at this particular stage in the development of American education the layman—or anybody else, for that matter—who feels the need for reform must necessarily be somewhat crotchety and cantankerous and devoted to negative
criticism, however distasteful it may be to play the crank. It
may be that those good old American bromides, "constructive
criticism" and "the spirit of cooperation" are somewhat less
than adequate weapons in the urgent task of the moment,
namely, the education of our citizenry in what is happening
in the public schools, which task is the essential preliminary
to ultimate reformation.

3. *The Selected Letters of Gustave Flaubert,* translated and
edited by Francis Steegmuller (New York; Farrar, Straus and
Young, Inc., 1953), p. 244.

I

The Decline in Learning

Professional educators, who have long scoffed at the "subject-centered curriculum" and emphasis on the Three R's, are now being goaded by their critics into claiming that even though subject matter no longer holds a primary position in the schools it is taught better than it ever was in the past. One professor of education makes the sweeping claim that repeated investigations "have proved that girls and boys in the public schools of the United States read better today, write more legibly, have greater competency in the arithmetical processes, and can outspell the young people of any other age."[1]

Lots of people who are not enemies of the public schools disagree with the professor and continue to take whacks at inadequacies in various subject fields. Edward Weeks, Jr., editor of the *Atlantic Monthly*, says that to him the evidence is overwhelming that the teaching of English in our high schools "has deteriorated to the point where the better-than-average graduates cannot write with accuracy, much less with skill."[2] This is confirmed by a friend of mine who teaches in

---

1. Herold C. Hunt, "Crisis in the Public Schools," in *Freedom and Public Education*, edited by Melby and Puner (New York; Frederick A. Praeger, 1953), p. 268.

2. *New York Herald Tribune*, June 15, 1952.

one of the great technical institutes which gets the cream of the crop of high school graduates; he tells me that of a dozen freshmen to whom he has recently acted as advisor all were badly in need of remedial work in spelling, grammar, and ordinary written expression. Oliver La Farge, after working with western undergraduates (who usually enter college on a high school certificate) had this to say:

> In a class of thirty, at least fifteen will dread what they call "essay exams." An essay exam is anything requiring written answers, as against checking off multiple choices or true-or-false statements on a prepared sheet. A quiz of ten questions requiring answers averaging fifty words apiece is feared; a major examination question, calling for several pages of answer, is a pure horror. The reason for this is clear in their contorted faces as they put pen to paper. It is painfully clear when one reads their exams. *They can't write....* They cannot spell, punctuation is quite beyond them, the mere formation of a written word troubles them.[3]

A teacher of commercial subjects at James Madison High School in New York City, Saul Bloch, after questioning the personnel managers of thirteen large business firms, reports that they were all pretty much in agreement that the average commercial graduate cannot do "mental arithmetic and simple fractions" and cannot use a dictionary "because they are not sufficiently familiar with the order of the letters in the alphabet and many do not know how to spell."[4] Maynard M. Boring, chairman of the Survey Committee of Engineers Joint Council, whose job it is to keep track of the supply and de-

3. "We Need Private Schools," *The Atlantic Monthly,* February, 1954.

4. *High Points,* publication of the New York City Board of Education, April, 1953.

mand of technical people, claims our public high schools are doing a poor job in elementary mathematical and scientific training, and quotes figures from the United States Office of Education to show that in the 28,000 high schools in this country, less than twenty per cent of the students take any mathematics beyond arithmetic, less than fifteen per cent take chemistry, less than five per cent physics.[5]

Dr. Frank J. Soday, director of research for the Chemstrand Corporation, speaking before the American Chemical Society, says that more and more companies are having to set up classes in reading, writing and mathematics so their new employees can get an adequate grounding in these basic subjects —and he was not talking about factory workers but graduate chemists.[6] Dr. W. E. Blackburn, head of the department of physical sciences at Murray State College in Kentucky, states that ninety-four college teachers of natural science in that state, on being questioned about the preparation of entering students in 1950–51, claimed that such students were deficient in ability to read, write, and speak English correctly; ability in arithmetic and algebra and natural science; and general academic preparation.[7]

President Harold W. Dodds of Princeton, in an unusually frank article (for heads of private institutions are naturally cautious in criticism of public education) reports that he finds a growing unrest "with the watered-down quality of basic learning which our youngsters are getting" in the public schools.[8] Gordon Keith Chalmers, president of Kenyon Col-

---

5. *U.S. News & World Report,* April 10, 1953.
6. Robert C. Cowen, "Three R's Taught to Technical Grads," *The Christian Science Monitor,* December 15, 1953.
7. *Ibid.*
8. "Your Youngster and the Public Schools," *The American Magazine,* January, 1954.

lege, says, "... the food of education has been softened down—nothing to bite on, with a deleterious effect upon the teeth of the mind. Genuine school mathematics is suffering a decline; languages are in eclipse; history has given way to programs of social reform. ..."[9]

Professor Harry J. Fuller of the University of Illinois says: "As one who is now embarking on his fifteenth year of university teaching, I am well acquainted with this decline in the quality of preuniversity training, and, since I first took chalk in hand, I have sadly observed the shrinking knowledge of spelling, arithmetic, English grammar, geography, history, and science in our freshmen."[10] Alfred S. Roberts, retiring as a high school principal after fifty years of service in New York City, said: "It is my considered judgment born of close contact with students and teachers that there has been, particularly during the last decade or so, grave deterioration in the intellectual training and work habits of our pupils. ..."[11]

In the interests of better articulation between school and college, the University of California makes it a standard practice to have conferences between freshmen and high school faculty representatives. Year after year the same complaints are made by the freshman regarding his preparation for college: "High school should be more thorough." "More mathematics and English composition needed." "Too easy in high school. Did not learn to study." "Give examinations which really require the student to know the subject." "High school

9. Report of a speech before the annual forum of the Tuition Plan, *School and Society*, April 3, 1954.

10. "The Emperor's New Clothes, or *Prius Dementat*," *The Scientific Monthly*, January, 1951.

11. "Along the Broad Way and the Side Lanes," *High Points*, June, 1953.

should have more writing." "Develop a better technique of study."[12]

But possibly I belabor the point, for my readers undoubtedly have their own evidences of the failure of modern schools in teaching the fundamentals. Professional educators are apt to scoff at such criticisms, anyway, as being subjective and unscientific, only conjecture and expressions of personal opinion; complaints of college professors about the poor quality of the students coming to them from the high schools and parental laments about the inability of children to read, write, and cipher, are apt to be dismissed as isolated, individual snap judgments, devoid of statistical significance. But when one examines the results of many of the surveys and statistical tables the educators are so fond of, private opinion in these matters is often startlingly confirmed. Here are some items picked almost at random:

A survey of English and speech instruction in New York City high schools showed that the number of retarded readers in the freshmen classes rose from twenty-six per cent in 1938 to thirty-four percent in 1947.[13]

On the other side of the continent, in Los Angeles, high school sophomores who took the Iowa Test in arithmetic in 1949 and 1950 had for both years a percentile score of eight, or in other words, ninety-two per cent of students tested nationally had higher scores. The ominous thing about this is that the same students ranked far above the national average in aptitudes, or general capacity for learning.[14]

---

12. *Freshman Views on Articulation,* University of California, Berkeley, January, 1949.

13. *School and Society,* January 3, 1953.

14. Information from the Los Angeles Board of Education supplied to the Citizens Schools Committee.

In 1951 a more dramatic example of the state of education in Los Angeles was revealed with the publication of results of a test "designed to contain only those items which the test makers felt to be the minimum that would be expected of pupils in the way of basic facts, knowledges, and skills." This test showed that eighteen per cent of 11,000 high school juniors didn't know how many months there are in a year; sixteen per cent were doubtful as to the cause for celebrating the Fourth of July; nine per cent didn't know how many three-cent stamps you can buy for seventy-five cents. And in view of the fact that sixty-two per cent of the students didn't know if the late Philip Murray, then much in the news, was a union leader or associated with the Standard Oil Company, there is possibly some question of the efficacy of the teaching of "current affairs," a field where the educators claim they are functioning with great effect. According to the press, when the associate superintendent in charge of curriculum was asked about these results, he replied: "We thought our methods were clicking fairly well. This test was an eye opener."[15]

A survey conducted by the Commerce and Industry Association of New York in cooperation with the Board of Education, found that 33,234 former high school students working in New York were ranked, on a percentage scale, as follows

15. *New York Herald Tribune*, November 29, 1951. In a form letter dated December 26, 1951, the associate superintendent did not affirm or deny the accuracy of the reports but in answer to apparently widespread criticism he made this somewhat less than crushing reply: "So far as are concerned the items widely published in newspapers, it is sufficient to say that those items were selected which appeared to have the greatest news value. Such deficiencies as became apparent from the testing are currently the subject of further study and action on the part of the Board of Education, the Superintendent, and the staff."

by their employers: reading, sixty-eight percent; writing, forty-five; arithmetic, forty-six; spelling, eighteen. A year later the association conducted a follow-up poll among employers to "determine what improvements, if any, have resulted during the last year and what further action is indicated. There was virtually none of the former and much of the latter."[16]

Over ten years ago the *New York Times* conducted its famous inquiry into the historical knowledge of college students, with startling results; among other discouraging items, it was discovered that twenty-five per cent of seven thousand students did not know that Lincoln was president during the Civil War; thirty per cent didn't know that Wilson was president during World War I; and eighty-four per cent couldn't think of two contributions Jefferson made to American thought and life. More recently the same newspaper made a survey of geographical knowledge among students with equally discouraging results.[17] (Proficiency in answering examination questions is not, of course, necessarily evidence of developed intelligence and is often the mark of the pedant; but to acknowledge this is far from discounting the value of examinations in determining how well the student is absorbing subject matter.)

Perhaps the most startling and disturbing information about the inadequacies of our schools come from the reports of Selective Service regarding the educational status of draftees during World War II and since. Although by 1940 practically all American youth remained in school long enough to acquire basic literacy, 716,000 men, or the equivalent in manpower of more than forty divisions, were rejected in World War II on

16. *New York Herald Tribune,* June 17, 1952 and May 31, 1953.
17. Edgar W. Knight, *Fifty Years of American Education* (New York; Ronald Press, 1952), p. 459.

grounds of mental deficiency, not mental disease. The greater number of these were not so much deficient in mentality as they were educationally undernourished. For almost fifteen years now the armed services have been complaining about the serious lack of educationally qualified men and about the necessity of setting up schools for them after they get in the service, schools aimed to provide them with nothing more elaborate than basic literacy. When the military has, in so many cases, been forced to repeat the work of the schools, one may legitimately ask how efficiently the latter are functioning.[18]

It is tempting to ascribe this decline in learning wholly to the evil influence of progressive education. Its responsibility for present conditions is indeed heavy. One of the primary flaws in the Deweyan philosophy, its failure to set up ends, its insistence that "the educational process has no end beyond itself"[19] and that the essence of education is no more than "vital energy seeking opportunity for effective exercise"[20]— which statements seem to imply that one experience is as good as any other—has undoubtedly had unfortunate classroom repercussions. As a corollary to this the progressives have often perverted the valid doctrine that the educational program ought to take account of the child's needs and interests into a mere catering to what the student thinks he wants. And the conception of discipline all too common to progressive education has sometimes amounted to an abandonment of adult responsibility for the guidance of youth.

---

18. See Eli Ginsberg and Douglas W. Bray, *The Uneducated* (New York; Columbia University Press, 1953).

19. John Dewey, *Democracy and Education* (New York; Macmillan, 1921), p. 59.

20. *Ibid.*, p. 84.

But because progressive education carries a heavy burden of sins I do not think we can use its back as a convenient place on which to pile all our present troubles. Many of the things going on in schools today seem to appall some progressives as much as they do traditionalists. The great debates between progressives and traditionalists during the 1920's and 30's, and to a lesser degree during the 40's, often involved fundamental philosophical principles, for while not all traditionalist educators were opposed to the relativism and pragmatism of Dewey and his followers others felt its consequences both in life and education to be almost disastrous; but for many the debate was largely over method and the practical question of what goes on in classrooms, the traditionalists believing in systematic organization of subject matter and formal discipline, the progressives relying on informal and improvised organization of subject matter and free activity. The traditionalists laid great stress on cultural heritage and the past as a guide to the present but so did many of the progressives; an extremist like William H. Kilpatrick might make a cult of the contemporaneous and talk as if everything that happened before 1900 was worthless, but it was John Dewey who said that "the achievements of the past provide the only means at command for understanding the present."[21] The best progressive schools of the 1920's, like North Shore Country Day in Winnetka, Lincoln in New York, or Shady Hill in Cambridge, whatever their unorthodoxies in method, taught a body of knowledge, as some of today's adults who graduated from them will point out, rather vehemently, when critics lump all progressive schools together.

The point I am making is that despite a sometimes funda-

---

21. Dewey, *Experience and Education* (New York; Macmillan, 1938), p. 93.

mental philosophical cleavage, the traditionalists and the modernists believed in content, in a body of subject matter to be taught, but parted company on matters of method. This is no longer the main debate in American education; the controversy today is between those who continue to believe that the cultivation of intelligence, moral as well as intellectual, is inextricably bound up with the cultural heritage and accumulated knowledge of humankind, and those who feel that education's primary task is to adjust the individual to the group, to see that he learns to respond "satisfactorily" to the stresses and strains of the social order. Ideally the two tasks are not mutually exclusive but the advocates of the latter consistently deride the former, engaging in a vigorous anti-intellectualism and a belittling of, and contempt for, content in education.[22]

Today there are two fashionable theories of the purpose of the school, Life Adjustment and Social Reconstruction, both of which may borrow the methods and techniques of the progressives but are far from commanding the allegiance or re-

22. While the main battle in education is no longer over method, I do not mean to imply that the progressives do not still wage lively, and sometimes delightfully absurd, skirmishes in behalf of method. A case is at hand from a recent yearbook of the John Dewey Society in which a lady professor of education tells how for twelve years she asked thousands of teachers who taught about Mesopotamia in geography classes how many had ever gone to Mesopotamia and how many intended to go. The answer was always the same, no one had been and no one expected to go, "yet without suitable personal experiences these teachers were trying to teach children by following facts discovered by others—facts logically organized but psychologically unsound for the young learner." Which is the equivalent of saying that you can't teach the facts about the Civil War unless you fought in it, or the facts about Mount Everest until you've climbed it. See "Subject-Matter Interpretations," by Ruth Streitz, *The American Elementary School* (New York; Harper & Brothers, 1953).

spect of all advocates of progressive education. I shall deal presently with the less entrenched of the two theories, Social Reconstruction, which defines the job of the school as indoctrination. For the moment, let us look at Life Adjustment which is now riding the crest of the wave of popularity in educational circles.

II

Adjustment Replaces Education

The Life Adjustment movement is not new, it is but an old acquaintance going under a newly assumed name. It is the latest manifestation of the idea that the school's task is only incidentally to train the intelligence and impart knowledge, that its real function is to serve as a gigantic bureau of social services where the attempt will be made to adjust the student to all "real life problems." Its importance derives from two factors: it echoes and in a sense sums up what public school educators have been advocating for twenty years; and it has semiofficial, even quasi-governmental sanction.

One dedicated advocate of Life Adjustment asks, "Who does not thrill to see the leaders who marched in the vanguard of this crusade?" Apparently Quintilian, Luther, Rousseau, Jefferson, Ben Franklin, Horace Mann, and Henry Barnard, among others, were practicing Life Adjusters. He then makes what seems to be an accurate statement regarding its present standing among schemes of educational "reform":

> In its present form this movement has outgrown every other movement of educational discontent; it out-heralds any other movement ever conceived; it is the first movement which has at one and the same time enlisted the energy, faith, and encouragement of educators at all levels; national, state, and local. This is different from what happened with the work of the NEA Committees, with the pronouncements of colleges and professors, or

of professional groups. It has strength; its organization is well conceived; its possibilities are great enough to challenge all professional persons at all levels.[1]

The movement originated on the highest "level," in the United States Office of Education, which office was then part of the Federal Security Agency and is now a division of the Department of Health, Education, and Welfare. In 1947 the Commissioner of Education appointed a Commission on Life Adjustment Education for Youth, and eventually this body came forth with a statement of purpose. Incidentally, one could hardly get a better illustration of the isolation of public school education from the world of learning and scholarship than the membership composition of this Commission. When the (then) Commissioner of Education, presumably the moral if not the official leader of American education, decides that the time has arrived "to effect major improvements in the programs and processes of secondary education" one might reasonably suppose that the commission appointed for studying the problem would include some outstanding scholars and authorities in subject fields. A careful perusal of the ninety names comprising the list of "educational leaders" attending the original conference reveals administrators, professors of education, vocational- home economics- and agriculture-specialists, and various educational bureaucrats, but not a single representative of the liberal arts. This would seem to indicate quite clearly what the U.S. Office of Education thinks of the place of the liberal arts in effecting "major improvements" in secondary education.[2]

---

1. Adolph Unruh, "Life Adjustment Education—A Definition," *Progressive Education*, February, 1952.

2. U.S. Office of Education, *Life Adjustment Education for Every Youth,* Bulletin No. 22, 1951.

The Commission's statement of purpose is in most regards a far from revolutionary document for it simply restates the aims of education as they have appeared in the "statement of purposes" of innumerable other commissions and committees issued during the past few years. The Commission wants an education which will equip all American youth to live democratically as home members, workers, and citizens; it is concerned with ethical and moral living, mental and emotional health, wholesome recreational interests; it believes in the dignity of work and the importance of personal satisfactions and achievement; and it makes the regulation bow to "the importance of fundamental skills."[3] In other words, it is the usual hotchpotch of unexceptionable, vague clichés, and has the usual weaknesses of such statements in trying to be all-inclusive, as well as expressing an apparent unawareness that some purposes of the school are primary and others subsidiary.

But in one respect the statement of the Commission is a milestone in the history of American education for it implies baldly that the majority of American high school students are incapable either of being prepared for college or trained for vocations. The original resolution which suggested a life adjustment program states that twenty per cent of the high school population can be prepared for college and another twenty per cent trained vocationally but for the remaining sixty per cent administrators must devise a new program. "College preparation or training for skilled occupations is neither feasible nor appropriate" for this group, says the Commission.[4]

This is pretty revolutionary doctrine and would seem to imply that the majority of American youth—sixty per cent—

---

3. *Ibid.*, pp. 9–10.
4. *Ibid.*, p. 16, p. 19.

are so dull that all the school can attempt to do is to adjust them to their environment. Arthur Bestor has said that this statement, if true, invalidates most of the assumptions that have underlain American democracy, and "enthrones once again the ancient doctrine that a clear majority of the people are destined from birth to be hewers of wood and drawers of water."[5] That some advocates of Life Adjustment have faced up to this implication is shown by this reference from a professor of education: "The neglected group . . . lacking aroused interests or pronounced aptitudes (which is probably fortunate for a society having a large number of jobs to be done requiring no unusual aptitudes or interests) also lacks the drives which allow us to serve their brothers and sisters more easily."[6]

Just what is it that Life Adjustment is going to do for the sixty per cent which apparently fared so ill under more traditional school programs? The report, *Life Adjustment Education for Every Youth,* gives no indication that anything is going to be done to devise more efficient techniques for reaching this group with the values inherent in traditional subject matter, or that the Commission even believes there *are* any such values. The theme of the low educational aptitude of the majority is driven home throughout the report: Only a small minority can have any real understanding of abstract mathematics; few students will have either the ability or the need to write and speak with accuracy; and the report of a National Education Association subsidiary is quoted, with approval, to

---

5. Arthur E. Bestor, *Educational Wastelands* (Urbana; The University of Illinois Press, 1953), p. 82.

6. Edward K. Hankin, "The Crux of Life Adjustment Education," *Bulletin* of the National Association of Secondary-School Principals, November, 1953, p. 72.

the effect that "reading to comprehend newspapers and magazines reasonably well" is a worthy aim in teaching "the educationally neglected student."[7] The Commission feels that "teachers are enthusiastic about the subjects they teach . . . more interested in securing greater enrollments for their subjects than in adjusting subjects to meet the needs of girls and boys. . . . There are enormous pressures for teachers and principals to continue doing the things they do well even though these practices fail to meet the needs of many pupils."[8] All this would seem to be a backhanded way of saying that even though teachers are enthusiastic about their subjects and competent in teaching them, they might as well give up the effort as far as the sixty per cent is concerned for they can't take it.

What the Commission is interested in for the sixty per cent, and what is heavily emphasized throughout the report are "the general areas" of citizenship, family life, conservation, general occupational adjustment, consumer education, leisure time, and health. These are undeniably worthy things many of which in former, less enlightened times, would come up incidentally in teaching the various subjects, but the unmistakable implication is that they are now largely to replace the subjects and become the curriculum itself. The Life Adjuster quoted earlier says the new curriculum is going to consist of nine items: education for family living, consumer economics, citizenship, job information, ethical and moral living, physical and emotional health, training for world citizenship and statesmanship, and—bringing up the rear of the procession as usual—training in fundamental skills.[9]

---

7. *Life Adjustment Education for Every Youth*, pp. 80–82.
8. *Ibid.*, p. 11.
9. "Life Adjustment Education—A Definition."

If one is to judge by the amount of discussion it gets in professional journals, and the number of influential educators who have paid homage to it, Life Adjustment is here to stay. Actually, as I have said, it's been here for a long time under various aliases such as Core Curriculum, General Education, Common Learnings, and Social Living, and is substantially the same program the Educational Policies Commission and other commissions affiliated with the National Education Association have been turning up periodically for the last twenty years. Whatever the nomenclature, these "programs" are similar in aim in that they all abandon formal subject matter in favor of integration of all subject matter towards an over-all objective, towards what the educators like to call "dynamic, functional learning." Perhaps it may be salutary to examine some of these programs which are springing up in junior and senior high schools all over the country. Many educators feel they represent an inevitable trend in public education. If so, one must shudder for the future of American youth for these programs, no matter how much good will and sincerity may be behind them, are unfortunately almost unfailingly anti-intellectual, trivial and a caricature of genuine education.

Here, for example, is the report of a core program as carried on in the ninth grade in a Maryland high school.[10] The day is divided into six periods; in the morning the students study home economics (for the girls), shop (for the boys), physical education for three days of the week and music for the other two, and general mathematics and general science. (This program is probably even more meagre than it sounds for "general" mathematics and science are usually watered-down

---

10. This is reported in Harold Alberty, *Reorganizing the High-School Curriculum* (New York; Macmillan, Revised Edition, 1953).

courses containing little real nourishment.) The two after-
noon periods, totaling about 104 minutes, are devoted to
"core," this particular program revolving around the topic
"What Makes Us Tick," a unit for "study of human behavior
and relationships." (Other units used in the same school have
such titles as Life Can Be Beautiful, There Are No Robinson
Crusoes, Am I Getting My Money's Worth.) This being a
modern school everything is, of course, very democratic and
involved with group dynamics—before anything can be done
there must be "organization of personnel." Accordingly the
class elects a steering committee, consisting of a chairman,
vice-chairman, and secretary, and six subcommittees, these
latter to be responsible for each "problem area" to be discussed. These problem areas (if you are still following me)
were selected by the class and are as follows:

> What parents should expect of us and what we desire and expect
> of our parents.
> How we can get started in social activities in our own age
> groups.
> How to have a successful "date."
> What to do, according to the rules of etiquette, in certain embar-
> rassing situations.
> When we should give gifts on our own, separate from "the fam-
> ily" giving.
> How to entertain at parties and other social activities.

Most of the class activity seemed to be involved with item
number three—how to have a successful date. Listed among
the "outstanding examples" of the students' activities in ex-
ploring this subject were a dramatization of how to make a
date, a poll on "controversial date problems" which was given
to a group starting with the seventh grade and extending up
to the faculty, a group study of the cost of corsages which in-

volved practicing telephone calls and personal interviews in the class, and a study of how to have "party fun."

This program was "democratically evaluated" by the class itself, with the members deciding that "outcomes actually covered more growth than the objectives included"; among these outcomes was learning to work better in a group, appreciating the other fellow's contribution, learning to write a script, learning good telephone etiquette. The teacher felt the unit had resulted in sincere interest in improving oral and written skills, increased poise in and respect for proper boy-girl social relationships, and excellent growth in group cooperation.

This core program must not be thought to be atypical; on the contrary it is representative in spirit and method of programs being carried on in schools over the country. The book which reports it, *Reorganizing the High-School Curriculum*, gives the details of many others "based upon the persistent common needs, problems, and interests of youth." The "units" range from the sublime (studies of human rights and world peace) to the ridiculous (studies of "growing up" in which such items as these are considered: "How often should I change my clothing?" "What can I do to keep my teeth white and my skin soft?" "What can I do with my old-fashioned parents?" "What should I talk about on a date?" and, my favorite among these problems, "May I show how I feel with my water colors?")[11]

Another educationist tells us that Los Angeles County has

---

11. My favorite core unit is one used in the 10th grade in a Denver high school, "Orientation to the school building." One would suppose that this course could consist of a half-hour tour of the washrooms, laboratories, gymnasium, etc., but then one would be underestimating the ability of educators to inflate the simple into the complex.

developed a course (a course, no less!) in which various personal problems are "outlined carefully" including the problem of *How to be Attractive and Well Groomed*. Under this heading are discussed such matters as how to banish unwanted hair, and how to bathe for health and cleanliness. (What else one bathes for, deponent saith not.) Among further questions which come up for consideration in this "course" (and I'm not making this up) are the following: How do you pick up a handkerchief? How do you sit down properly at various occasions? How can you improve your stride and still maintain poise?[12] Thus is "real life education" carried on.

Another document, *Improving School Holding Power*, shows that in various cities, such as Rochester, St. Louis, St. Paul, Minneapolis, and Detroit, programs have been introduced in the schools which follow closely the reasoning of the Life Adjustment advocates. It is interesting to learn from this booklet how St. Paul has increased the holding power of its high schools; among other devices it has adjusted school work to individual differences, reduced drastically the percentage of failures, abandoned grade standards on report cards in favor of individual standards, and eliminated the practice of making satisfactory scholastic accomplishment a requirement for athletic and club activities. This fairly complete abandonment of all educational standards may help to keep young people in school; it is difficult to see how any reasonable person could claim that it comprises sound preparation for maturity.[13]

---

12. Leonard, *op. cit.*, pp. 342–43.

13. *Improving School Holding Power*, Circular No. 291, U.S. Office of Education, 1951. In the matter of holding power, I have long suspected that changing the curriculum has little to do with keeping young people in school, and am glad to have my suspicion

What the core and similar programs amount to is a sort of juvenile bull session. Conceivably many of the items discussed are of real concern to the students but to make the discussion of them the whole curriculum, or a major part of it, with the consequent necessary neglect of real subject matter, is to cheat the youth by neglecting the basic facts and disciplines which alone will enable him to arrive at mature judgments about his concerns. Many of the items could probably be more advantageously discussed in private conversation with the teacher or school counselor than in a group. Not the least unfortunate aspect of these programs is just this emphasis on the group and belittling of individuality. (The youth who wants to discuss with a committee what he should talk about on a date doesn't deserve to have a date.)

Reading such a book as *Reorganizing the High-School Curriculum* (which is considered authoritative in the field) one gets the impression that none of the reorganizing is going to be in the direction of improved teaching of subject matter but entirely in the direction of finding ways of undermining subject matter. Although the author laments the sparsity of core programs in American schools, another advocate assures us that "procedures involving at least something of these principles and their applications will be found not many years hence in practically all but the very small, weak high schools and the very large conservative ones."[14] Harl R. Douglass, who makes this prediction, states that progress will be slow

---

confirmed by an educationist who says that "only about one-fourth of those who discontinue say they do so because of the curriculum." See *The American Secondary School*, edited by Paul B. Jacobson (New York; Prentice-Hall, 1952), p. 120.

14. Harl R. Douglass, *Secondary Education for Life Adjustment of American Youth* (New York; Ronald Press, 1952), p. 184.

for a number of reasons including the fact that parents (those notorious stumbling blocks) are confused and have a tendency to believe that the new program is less valuable than "the good old-fashioned authoritarian, fear-motivated program that they followed in school."[15] (Modern educators like to pretend that all American schools of twenty or more years ago were modeled on Mr. Squeers' Dotheboys Hall.)

The anti-intellectual bias which animates advocates of these programs is expressed with unusual bluntness in a book called *New Schools for a New Culture* which is a report of another core program, this one carried on since 1937 at the Evanston Township High School, Evanston, Illinois.

> In the school of tomorrow [say the authors of this report] the aristocratic, cultural tradition of education must be completely and finally abandoned. Scholarship must become functional. This does not mean that it will be concerned only with the material wants of man or that it will lack creativeness or intellectual stimulation, but it *will* cease to rattle the bones of the dead past solely for pleasure or, worse, out of a sense of academic duty. . . .
>
> Any help we can give them (those who possess unusual intellectual curiosity) should be theirs, but such favored people learn directly from their surroundings. Our efforts to teach them are quite incidental in their development. It is therefore unnecessary and futile for the schools to attempt to gear their programs to the needs of unusual people. . . .
>
> Teachers have thought they must clothe themselves with the robes of the scholar and perpetuate the scholarly tradition so far as possible in every one of their pupils.
>
> The school of tomorrow must accept in fact that general education in a democracy must be for the masses.[16]

15. *Ibid.*, p. 185.
16. Charles M. MacConnell, Ernest O. Melby, Christian O. Arndt, Leslee J. Bishop, *New Schools for a New Culture* (New York; Harper & Brothers, Revised Edition, 1953), pp. 154–55.

Some of the argument in this statement is hard to follow, possibly because the authors have themselves abandoned that part of the cultural tradition which emphasizes lucid expression. Do they mean that any large part of scholarship is concerned with rattling the bones of the dead past, and if they do mean this, is it true? What do they mean by the airy reference to the "dead" past—isn't all the past alive as it illumines the present? And if scholars get pleasure out of rattling the bones, isn't that functional? In the long run isn't the function and purpose of all education to increase man's pleasure by increasing his knowledge and understanding? And do they really mean to say that unusual people learn directly from their surroundings but that it is futile for the schools to provide the surroundings that will ... them in their development?

Aside from these ambiguities, it seems clear enough that they have a strong animus against education as a means of transmitting the intellectual and cultural tradition of the race, that they think it is foolish for a teacher of the masses to attempt to be a scholar, and that it is also foolish for a teacher to try to hold all students to some standard of scholarship.

A few pages further on in their book the authors strike another blow for the new schools in a new culture:

It is well that the schoolmaster's efforts to make scholars of all who come to him have never met with conspicuous success. The world's work is not done from an armchair. . . . The work of the world is accomplished through intelligent and skillful action. The school of tomorrow must recognize this both by its emphasis and by its acceptance. Scholarship, we repeat, must become functional in human affairs, even though a place may be allowed a few scholars who concern themselves with what they call "pure learning."[17]

---

17. *Ibid.*, p. 162.

One fears that that implied sneer in their reference to pure learning bodes ill for those poor scholars who are going to apply to the educational commissars of the future to be "allowed" to pursue their armchair specialties. And one might well ask whether intelligent and skillful action appears full-blown out of the void or does it have its wellsprings in the discipline of intellectual and scholarly preparation? One would suppose that some armchair thinking would have to precede action, even in the new schools and the new culture.

It is interesting to see how the authors' anti-intellectual bias applies to a concrete subject such as written expression. They want, of course, the "simpler type" of writing "which meets the needs of the average citizen." It turns out that "writing is not learned through previous instruction. It is learned functionally *by writing when and what* one needs to write." But there are two nasty enemies lying in wait for the student, the professor in college and the future employer; the former sets artificial standards which students have to meet for college entrance, and the latter, being a good deal of a snob, foolishly accepts the professor's standards and demands them in his employees. "Such," sigh our authors, "are the values established by the intellectual aristocracy in America."[18]

One can imagine the difficulties the good student in the academic sense is going to have in the schools of tomorrow. Our authors say that the child who has learned to follow rules at home is often an honor student in a school "that has for its chief objective the preparation of assigned lessons" so he is naturally going to be ill at ease when he goes to a school which abjures this objective. They readily admit he is going to be confused, and faced with the necessity of "remaking in four years a whole habit pattern" in which he has had years

18. *Ibid.*, pp. 39–40.

34

of conditioning, but fortunately the new teachers in the new school are willing to take on this "discouraging assignment" and "do with it as much as we are able."[19] In other words, although they can't guarantee anything, they will do their best to undermine any tendencies in new students towards academic accomplishment. This is a logical position for such determined equalitarians as the authors; an aristocracy of the intellect cannot be tolerated where intellectual matters are themselves held in contempt.

The casual reader wading through the involuted prose of *New Schools for a New Culture,* especially the reader who is out of touch with public school matters, may be inclined to think that the dreary viewpoint expressed therein is that of a small minority, or lunatic fringe, and in any case is only presentation of theory. To speak of the last supposition first, it should be borne in mind that the objectives are now being carried out in the core program of the Evanston Township High School which removes the authors' ideas from the realm of the merely theoretical. Secondly, far from being a scheme of a fringe group, it is sponsored by high priests in the hierarchy of American education. One of the authors of the book, Ernest O. Melby, was formerly dean of the School of Education at Northwestern University which school helped to organize the program, and is now dean of the School of Education at New York University, one of the largest and most influential such schools in the country. Dean Melby is an important figure in education by virtue of his position alone but his importance is further emphasized by the frequency with which he manages to get his viewpoint expressed not only in professional but also in lay journals. The point of view expounded in *New Schools for a New Culture* may be nonsense,

19. *Ibid.*, pp. 122–123.

dangerous nonsense, but it is not inconsequential for it is uttered by respected and influential men in the educational world and has been translated into a going experiment in an actual public school.

The revolt against "intellectual aristocracy" reached its logical end when a principal of a junior high school publicly advocated abandoning the attempt to teach everyone to read. This quotation, from a paper written in 1951, has appeared widely but deserves reiteration as a warning of what American public school education may come to:

> Through the years we've built a sort of halo around reading, writing, and arithmetic. We've said they were for everybody . . . rich and poor, brilliant and not-so-mentally endowed, ones who liked them and those who failed to go for them. Teacher has said that these were something "everyone should learn." The principal has remarked, "All educated people know how to write, spell and read." When some child declared a dislike for a sacred subject, he was warned that, if he failed to master it, he would grow up to be a so-and-so.
>
> The Three R's for All Children, and All Children for the Three R's! That was it.
>
> We've made some progress in getting rid of that slogan. But every now and then some mother with a Phi Beta Kappa award or some employer who has hired a girl who can't spell stirs up a fuss about the schools . . . and ground is lost. . . .
>
> When we come to the realization that not every child has to read, figure, write and spell . . . that many of them either cannot or will not master these chores . . . then we shall be on the road to improving the junior high curriculum.
>
> Between this day and that a lot of selling must take place. But it's coming. We shall some day accept the thought that it is just as illogical to assume that every boy must be able to read as it is that each one must be able to perform on the violin, that it is no more reasonable to require that each girl shall spell well than it is that each shall bake a good cherry pie. . . .

If and when we are able to convince a few folks that mastery of reading, writing and arithmetic is not the one road leading to happy, successful living, the next step is to cut down the amount of time and attention devoted to these areas in general junior high-school courses. . . .[20]

Here again, this blithe, and one might say frightening, contempt for learning cannot be dismissed as isolated, personal eccentricity. The paper from which these quotations are taken was read before the country's largest professional association of public high school principals and was published in that association's official journal, and not as a horrible example, either. It would be absurd to suggest that all educationists subscribe to these views but the fact that they could be delivered to a professional association charged with the education of American youth and go unrebuked confirms one's suspicions that the educationists are more concerned with decrying the critics who accuse education of being anti-intellectual than they are with rebuking their own members whose remarks are flagrant proof of the charge.

The life adjustment-core curriculum-common learnings people continue their efforts to undermine those colleges which still demand that a student who seeks entrance should present some evidence of exposure to the intellectual disciplines in high school. The U.S. Office of Education reports, with satisfaction, that in one state 121 high schools and thirty-eight colleges have signed an agreement according to which the colleges will "disregard the pattern of subjects of high-school graduates who are recommended for college entrance." The high schools' part of the agreement consists of a vague prom-

20. A. H. Lauchner, "How Can the Junior High School Curriculum Be Improved?" *Bulletin* of the National Association of Secondary-School Principals, March, 1951, pp. 299–300.

ise to improve "guidance procedures" and "to carry on continuous efforts to improve curriculum programs."[21] In some educationist circles the argument is no longer over the amount or quality of intellectual training; the question has been resolved by frank proposals to abandon entirely intellectual disciplines as such in high school. Here is a quotation from Harl R. Douglass, an influential and prolific Life Adjuster who is also director of the College of Education at the University of Colorado:

> In the early days of secondary and higher education in the United States, Latin and Greek were the subjects required for college entrance. A little later, mathematics, including arithmetic, was required. Still later, instruction in English and in science was added, and, in the latter part of the nineteenth century, a year of history. However valuable the study of these preferred subjects was for the purpose of preparing pupils for college curricula and college teaching as it existed in the seventeenth and eighteenth centuries or perhaps in the early part of the nineteenth century, it became increasingly questionable that the subjects most commonly required for college entrance made any unique or greatly superior contribution to the work of young people in college.[22]

I have read over this quotation several times and have come to the conclusion that, incredible as it may seem, the author means what he says, viz., that though, for entrance, colleges require preparation in mathematics, English, science, and history, such preparation is of no value to the student

---

21. *Vitalizing Secondary Education*, Bulletin No. 3, Report of the First Commission on Life Adjustment Education for Youth, Reprinted 1954, U.S. Department of Health, Education and Welfare, p. 58.
22. Douglass, *op. cit.*, p. 531.

when he gets to college. That this interpretation is the correct one seems to be confirmed by another remark of the author's:

> An increasing number of theorists and administrators are advocating that, except possibly for a very few bright students, the study of foreign languages should be postponed to the college years. There are also some, and their number is slowly increasing, who hold a similar position with respect to the traditional courses in mathematics. These hold that algebra, geometry, and trigonometry have relatively little value except as college preparation or except for a few college curricula, and that therefore most of the instruction in those fields should be postponed until college.[23]

Because of the forces of reaction and entrenched custom, Dr. Douglass realizes that the happy day when the main body of subject matter may be dispensed with must be postponed, but in the meantime he has some practical suggestions for emasculating the content of subject matter. In the interests of making English "more meaningful" than in the past he suggests that it be organized into "idea-centered" units where the pupils "would be thrown into active language situations that would force them to discuss, to report findings, to interview, to take part in conversations, to write letters, to summarize reports, to take notes, and to write imaginatively about their own experiences." One would suppose that pupils would need some knowledge of the rules and structure of language to perform these tasks but Dr. Douglass assures us that just *doing* them does more to "establish comfort and proficiency in language than the work in grammar and usage that formerly dominated our courses of study." He does admit that the teacher may have to give some initial help so the

---

23. *Ibid.*, p. 598.

pupils may "avoid language difficulties that they may get into," but such help may be given "through a nontechnical, thought approach to language problems not based on formal grammatical terminology." One may be puzzled as to what a "nontechnical, thought approach" may be but we are informed that three other professors of education have found it not only more "efficient" but "more economical in time" than traditional training in English usage.[24]

One of the professors to whom Dr. Douglass refers, John DeBoer of the University of Illinois, suggests that the school should make the effort to "cultivate more than one kind of English—the kind which is natural and comfortable and intelligible in the students' own group, and the kind which may have a much wider range of acceptability in English-speaking countries." These "levels of usage" are to be learned through "abundant uses" and through instruction based on "grounds of social practice" rather than through "systematic study *about* language." "Grammar is for editorial use by the advanced student."[25] I have not seen *Teaching Secondary English,* a volume of which Professor DeBoer is coauthor, but can imagine it must be a novel treatment of the subject.

Three more professors of education who look kindly on Life Adjustment and have written an influential textbook for teachers, find a new reason for belittling spelling and grammar:

> The teaching of spelling and grammar may contribute very little, if anything, to the realization of democratic ideals—except as these skills may be required by a few persons for vocational purposes and thus for their well-being in society, as in the case

---

24. *Ibid.,* pp. 343, 344.
25. John DeBoer, "The Teaching of Communication," *Progressive Education,* May, 1952.

of teachers and clerical workers. On the other hand, mastery of the habits of effective thinking and critical reading and listening is to be rated high on the scale of objectives that satisfy the democratic ideals. For democracy is based on the principle that the common man can manage public, as well as private, affairs if he has a chance to acquire information and to learn to think for himself.[26]

How the common man is going to manage his "critical reading" without benefit of spelling or the rules of the English language, or where he is going to acquire habits of effective thinking, or the literacy, that will enable him to manage public affairs, the authors do not state; nor, for that matter, do they tell us why the teacher should bother to learn spelling and the rules of grammar if she is only to teach them to other teachers, and clerks. In this connection, they set up a stern test to measure the usefulness of written expression. (Personal satisfaction and pleasure therein, of course, has nothing to do with it.)

> No amount of past usefulness . . . can assure the value of subject matter for today. . . . Persons who believe that more emphasis should now be placed upon the study of grammar—on the ground that in the past such study has produced better written expression—must show that the social importance of good written expression is as great today as in the last century, when grammar played a dominant role in the school's program.[27]

Perhaps the people of the British Isles might testify to the social importance of Winston Churchill's written and spoken

---

26. B. Othanel Smith, William O. Stanley, J. Harlan Shores, *Fundamentals of Curriculum Development* (Yonkers; World Book Company, 1950), p. 265.

27. *Ibid.*, p. 287.

expression during the dark days of World War II. Churchill was not a brilliant student but he has spoken many times of his gratefulness to his schoolmasters in the English language for their persistency in keeping him to a task he disliked. I doubt if they, or any good teacher of any subject at any time, gave too much thought to the "social importance" of the subject but were content to believe that if education can produce a good *man* the social will take care of itself.

But let us return to Dr. Douglass and see what he has to say about the teaching of foreign languages. Here he is aware of the complications arising from lack of training in formal grammar but his ideal seems to be a "more functional, immediately practical" knowledge of a foreign language—which apparently does not include the ability to speak it correctly. Some of the "offerings" in foreign language courses which he approves are courses in world literature (in translation), special commercial courses, and short-unit courses in "traveler's Spanish."[28] (One may be permitted to feel for the traveler when he discovers that Spanish speaking people don't speak traveler's Spanish.)

Dr. Douglass, of course, is against "verbalism." He claims that the high school education of the past was largely a matter of learning words and that the teacher accepted as evidence of learning the pupil's ability to repeat words found in the textbooks. (What good teacher in any age ever adopted such a method?) The educators are slowly solving the problem of providing "more meaningful and more vividly interesting experiences" but Dr. Douglass feels that "the problem has become somewhat accentuated . . . by increased dependence of young people upon pictures in comics, in movies, and in tele-

---

28. Douglass, *op. cit.*, pp. 352, 353, 354.

vision." Then he adds that "the solution to this problem may be accelerated" by more training of teachers "with respect to the use of audiovisual aids and community research."[29] I think this means that now that we have given up reading, the job of the teacher is to find superior pictures for the pupils to look at. The "community research" part of it, I suspect, would be good old Field Trips to the mayor's office and the county courthouse, interviewing merchants and social workers, etc.

Throughout his long book the author shows only impatience or scorn for those who insist that education must continue to be concerned with matters of the intellect and that it ought to have a body of subject content. He also consistently caricatures and misrepresents traditional schools to the point where the reader wonders how anybody who went to school before the coming of Life Adjustment managed to learn anything or survived the barbaric procedures of those schools. (Here is one horrible example of the evils of the schools of yesterday: "Such procedures as learning to obey the teacher and trying to learn things which were not understood and difficult were considered good mental and moral training."[30] Just think of anybody ever having had the idea that obeying the teacher and trying to learn something difficult was good training! It's hard to remember how antediluvian schools used to be before the educationists took over.)

Again, I feel the necessity of pointing out that Dr. Douglass is hardly an isolated phenomenon. He is the director of a teacher training institution and exerts influence far beyond his school and small state by the great number of education textbooks he has written, books used widely in the education of future teachers. He was also one of the chosen ninety who

29. *Ibid.*, p. 603.
30. *Ibid.*, p. 476.

attended the original conference, called by the Commissioner of Education, which set up the Life Adjustment program.

If you are appalled by the picture he draws of the new and meaningful curriculum of the future you may be cheered by a couple of regretful admissions he has to make. You may be glad to know that "how to get rid of the conventional report card" and substitute one "less likely to stimulate parents to unwise attempts to provide incentives to better efforts" remains an unsolved problem.[31] Perhaps even more hopeful is his rueful admission that, despite all the advances we have made towards "a modern concept of objectives" and despite the professed theory of teachers and principals, "visits to the classrooms unmistakably reveal practices based on the assumption that there is subject matter to be taught."[32]

If enough teachers can maintain such an idiosyncrasy perhaps public school education may yet survive the onslaught of the Life Adjusters.

31. *Ibid.*, p. 608.
32. *Ibid.*, p. 597.

III

Adjustment Replaces Education
(continued)

Perhaps the reader unversed in current educational philosophy will feel that in the foregoing pages I have, for the sake of making my point about the deleterious effect of Life Adjustment, been highly selective in my quotations. I assure him that I have not. Almost any of the books on curriculum revision which have appeared in the past fifteen or twenty years advocate the same "reforms" as these authors from whom I have been quoting. So do members of departments of education in the various states.[1] During the past twenty years many educational commissions have presented reports on secondary education; most of them—the Harvard report was a notable exception—explicitly or implicitly state the same conclusions that are now reached by the Commission on Life Adjustment Education for Youth. Stripped of their usual verbiage these reports seem more or less in agreement on two points: (1) a large segment of American youth,

---

1. See, for example, the pamphlet "The Redirection, Reorganization, and Retooling of Secondary Education," issued by the Connecticut State Department of Education (1944). As this is a pioneer statement of the principles and aims of Life Adjustment it is not surprising that its author, Paul D. Collier, became first chairman of the Commission on Life Adjustment Education for Youth.

probably the majority, is incapable of absorbing education as we have known it in the past, and (2) a program of "adjustment" must be devised which will keep this large segment contented for four years in high school. Dr. Douglass, our Life Adjuster from the last chapter, goes even further and states that this program should be for everyone, not only for those who can't take something better:

> While the movement [the Life Adjustment movement] was aimed especially at the development of a modern functional program of secondary education for those who will not go either (1) to college or (2) into occupations for which they can be trained specifically in high school, estimated to consist nationally of 60 per cent of high school boys and girls, it is coming to be believed by more and more people that a good program for that 60 per cent *might well be an excellent program for all American youth.* [Italics mine.][2]

There's a noble ideal to aim at—mediocrity, or worse, for all. Instead of trying to reduce the ranks of the sixty per cent, let's be democratic and bring the other forty per cent down to the same level. The Commission on Life Adjustment Education for Youth seems to agree with Dr. Douglass for it states that "life adjustment education is for all, even though there is a special concern for the so-called sixty per cent."[3]

It is ironic that the current skepticism of the ability of the majority to "take" education comes not from those who are supposed to believe in an "aristocratic" education but from professional educators who are apt to make a fetish of democracy and equalitarianism. There is an old tradition that the majority of Americans aren't very bright—H. L. Mencken

2. Douglass, *op. cit.*, p. 170.
3. *Vitalizing Secondary Education*, p. 35.

called them "boobs" and "yokels," Albert Jay Nock thought
them "subhuman," and the advertising agencies seem to put
them at about the high-grade moron level—but it is somewhat
surprising to observe this assumption becoming a plank in the
reform platform of educators. Watching Americans at their
devotions, reading comics or looking at television, or observ-
ing how easily they can be sold a product or a fad or how susceptible they are to propaganda, one would perhaps be fool-
hardy to defend their collective intelligence; but the folly of
overestimating it seems to me to be less dangerous than the
results of assuming its low quality.

I will return to the problem of what are apt to be the consequences when we assume the majority of our fellows to be
fools or dullards, but for the moment perhaps we might look
at the American intelligence when measured by the tests educators have themselves devised. According to an article by
the Parent and Child Editor of the *New York Times,* only 16
per cent of American children between the ages of 3–14 are
below average in intelligence, that is, with I.Q.'s below 90.
Sixty-eight per cent are in the I.Q. range of 90–110 (called
normal or average) and 15 per cent are in the above-average
range of 110–135, while one per cent are in the gifted category
of over 135.[4] If these figures are at all accurate (and if we
accept intelligence tests as a not infallible but rough indication of native intelligence) there is little justification for the

---

4. Dorothy Barclay, "Handling High I.Q.'s, *The New York
Times Magazine,* November 22, 1953. While there is not precise
agreement among psychologists and testers in regard to national
intelligence averages there does seem to be general agreement that
at least 60 per cent fall in the average (90-110) category. This is
the figure, for instance, given in "The Concept of Intelligence,"
by Albert R. Lang, in the volume *Twentieth Century Education*
(New York; Philosophical Library, 1946), p. 240.

contention of the Life Adjusters that 60 per cent of American youth are incapable of either college preparation or learning a trade. Before they released their figures they should have consulted the report of another government-sponsored body, the President's Commission on Higher Education, which estimated that 49 per cent of the population has the mental ability to complete fourteen years of schooling in general, and vocational, studies and that at least 32 per cent has the ability to complete advanced liberal or specialized education.[5]

There is no doubt that in any one classroom there will be a wide range of intelligence among the pupils, presenting to the teacher perplexing problems in method, but nothing will be solved by the device of abandoning real education for those who are less facile with ideas. Certainly the high school curriculum needs to be reorganized and improved but the efforts of the professional educators in this direction never seem to touch the great major problem, viz., how to reach the less gifted with the values inherent in subject matter, especially English and history. Their efforts all seem bent on doing away with these subjects or "integrating" and watering them down to the point where all substance and value is squeezed out. I don't know how this major problem is going to be solved but certainly the teaching profession as a whole ought to be ad-

---

5. *Higher Education for American Democracy*, A Report of the President's Commission on Higher Education, 1948, p. 41. This Commission had its own anti-intellectual bias. See p. 32: "We shall be denying educational opportunity to many young people as long as we maintain the present orientation of higher education toward verbal skills and intellectual interests." What kind of higher education would be devoid of intellectual interests? Perhaps the Commission is using the term higher in the simple sense of being above the elementary and high schools.

dressing themselves to its solution. If we expect the boy with an I.Q. of 90 to become a citizen and make the judgments required of a citizen we ought to be busy devising ways of making him understand the ideas which have shaped his country and world and we ought to be teaching him how to "communicate" intelligibly. Perhaps if we succeed in inculcating these major learnings we can trust him to find out for himself what to talk about on a date and how often to change his clothing.

But to return to the basic assumption of the educators that the majority of Americans aren't very bright and therefore cannot be educated in the traditional sense but need to be adjusted to the group, we ought to ask ourselves what are the practical results of such an assumption. One of the immediately recognizable results is that such an assumption tends to turn the educative process into primarily a group rather than an individual affair; it is not the person who matters but the team and its welfare. As the authors of *New Schools for a New Culture,* quoted earlier, have said, "it is futile for the schools to attempt to gear their programs to the needs of unusual people"; education in a democracy "must be for the masses." The "unusual people" are left to shift for themselves, or as Harl Douglass suggests, the program for the masses "might well be an excellent program for all American youth."

American educational theory tends more and more towards this mass conception, towards a system where the ideal is identical experience, where deviation from the commonalty is frowned upon. In this connection, I have seen a letter from the state department of education in one of our large states, informing parents who planned to teach their child at home that they would not under the law be permitted to do so, even though there was no question of the competency of the parents to teach. The department's reason for this decision is interesting:

> No matter how competent the parents may be, the child who obtains his schooling at home is not having an experience equivalent to that of the child who goes to an authorized school. The school program does not consist only of mastering the 3 R's and the various content subjects. Perhaps the most important part of the school program is the association in a group. . . . Practically all American living today is a cooperative affair. Children have to learn to take turns and to share. Group discipline and group loyalties have to be developed.

No one would argue that the state does not have the right to hold parents responsible for seeing that their children receive an education, but this statement advances an entirely novel conception in American law in relation to education, i.e., that the state has the right to demand that children be educated in groups and conditioned to group discipline and group loyalties. That this could be adopted as the official stand of one of our large states shows how easily and complacently we are drifting into a rigid educational conformity.

Another example of the growing impatience among educators with nonconformity is the opposition to private schools, even though only roughly eight per cent of youth attend private and parochial schools in this country. I would like to consider this opposition for a moment for it is bound up with the present ideological conflict in American education.

Parents send their children to private schools for a variety of reasons. Some do so because they feel there is social prestige attached to private school attendance; some think the chances of inculcating manners and the social graces are greater; some have religious reasons; some feel the private school educates better than the available public school. In some cases probably a combination of these reasons applies but there would seem to be small doubt that the last reason is in most cases the decisive one; in the vast majority of cases parents are motivated by the desire to secure for their children what they consider a superior education.

In any case, one would suppose that the principle of the right of parents to send their children to the school of their choice was well established, especially among those who like to lecture the rest of us about the "dynamics of democracy," but it is sometimes surprising how reluctantly this principle is accepted. Occasionally a voice is raised which suggests that maybe private schools are all right but they had better watch their step. How else is one to interpret Professor Sidney Hook's statement that the right to receive education in *addition* to that provided by the public schools is essential to democratic educational policy but that the "right to receive education in private schools from partisan agencies as a *substitute* for public education" may be, under certain circumstances, "an overt threat to democracy?"[6] Does this mean that a democratic educational policy will only sanction ancillary private schools or will full-time private schools be permitted which have proved themselves—and to what body?—nonpartisan? Mr. Hook does not explain what he means by "partisan agencies" or under what circumstances they constitute an "overt threat" but in view of his well-known antipathy to all religion save the religion of democracy, perhaps one is justified in suspecting that his partisan agencies might turn out to be church schools, or even nondenominational schools

6. *Education for Modern Man* (New York; Dial Press, 1946), p. 39.

which cannot bring themselves to the complete divorce of education and religion which seems to be Mr. Hook's ideal. I think that what Mr. Hook is really saying is that you can do whatever you want with your child, educationally, as long as he puts in full time in official, state-sponsored schools.

Former President James Bryant Conant of Harvard, who has become a vigorous opponent of the expansion of private schools, is convinced that they are a threat to unity in our American life. Says he: "The greater the proportion of our youth who fail to attend our public schools and who receive their education elsewhere, the greater the threat to democratic unity." "If one wished generation after generation to perpetuate class distinction based on hereditary status in a given society, one would certainly demand a dual system of schools. . . . A dual system serves and helps to maintain group cleavages, the absence of a dual system does the reverse. This is particularly true of secondary schools."[7]

Mr. Conant is so convinced of the importance of the American public school "as an instrument for strengthening the spirit of national unity" he is willing to argue with parents that this social function outweighs any possible drawbacks arising from the school's inefficiency in carrying out its primary function of promoting moral values and providing a good education.

If they (parents) have doubts about the ability of secular schools to promote the growth of moral and spiritual values, then these doubts must be weighed against the advantages of a pupil's attending a free school for all denominations. Similarly, if a family questions the ability of the local high school to pre-

7. *Education and Liberty* (Cambridge; Harvard University Press, 1952), pp. 81–82.

pare a gifted boy or girl adequately for university work (and the question unfortunately must be raised in many communities today), the family will have to balance these misgivings against the advantage of mixing with all sorts of people while at school.[8]

In other words, parents whose son's sense of moral values may be blunted can say to each other, "Ah, yes, but it's a non-denominational, democratic blunting, free for all"; and parents whose daughter may not be learning anything in school can always console each other by saying, "But how nice that she can mix with all sorts of people." This attitude of Mr. Conant's betrays a wholly social conception of education; it implies that the purpose of education is not cultivation of the individual's moral and ethical and intellectual perceptions but adjustment to the group in the interests of an undefined "unity." It is one more piece of evidence, and from an influential source, of the modern educator's preoccupation with the person not as a person, but as a sociological specimen.

One might well ask what is this "unity" on behalf of which Mr. Conant is willing to sacrifice youth? Why isn't the healthy system to have diversity in our unity? Don't adults who have gone to both private and public schools quite frequently manage to cooperate in public service, both locally and nationally? Anyone who has ever served on a committee or engaged in a community activity (and this must include just about every adult American) knows that the answer to that last question is in the affirmative. It is perhaps not unity we need, or certainly not unity based on the artificial criterion of attendance at the same school; this kind of test supposes erroneously that just being together produces unity. What we need is a sense of community and we get that only when per-

8. *Ibid.*, p. 83.

sons associating together, whether they be from public or private schools, have learned some of the things appropriate to all men. To think you can balance "the growth of moral and spiritual values" and adequate preparation for university work against "the advantage of mixing with all sorts of people" and grant the edge to the latter is simply to "make a strong pull and a long pull and a pull all together for the sake of togetherness," as Santayana thought Billy Phelps' Yale was doing.

Both Mr. Conant and Mr. Hook think we are getting diversity in our public education because politically we are still committed to the concept of local responsibility for our schools. As far as boards of education are concerned I think this concept of local responsibility is fast becoming a myth; the boards may still exercise responsibility as plant managers but it is becoming increasingly clear that the American public school is rapidly becoming a monolithic structure as far as what goes on in the schools in the way of learning is concerned. This is no longer, in the large sense, being decided at the local level at all but by the professors of education and their satellites in the state departments of education as I shall try to show in a later chapter.

At best a sociological theory of the aims of education is apt to produce docile individuals animated by a desire for group conformity and social solidarity, qualities admirable, perhaps, in an army but considerably less admirable in potentially free human beings. But the sociological theory of education can turn in another direction than acceptance of and adjustment to current social mores—in quite the opposite direction, as a matter of fact. If the majority of American youth is dull and hence malleable, why can't doctrinaires, if they can achieve strategic positions, mold youth in any desired shape, towards any ideology? The twentieth century, which has witnessed an increasing disregard for the individual, has been the great period of human manipulation when diabolical, or merely clever men, have devised ways of inducing the masses to accept a new ideology, or a new commercial product. It is unreasonable to expect that organized education should escape this itch for manipulation, nor has it, as we shall now see when we turn to consideration of the school of thought in education known as Social Reconstruction.

IV

Educational Brain-washing, Democratic Style

The theory that the task of the schools is to indoctrinate pupils in behalf of a new social, economic, and political order and that the teacher must therefore be a propagandist as well as a teacher, was a good deal more popular (at least openly) in this country twenty years ago than it is today. This is understandable enough to those who remember the political and cultural atmosphere of the early thirties when it seemed that the majority of intellectuals felt that capitalism and individualism were doomed and that a controlled economy and some sort of political collectivism constituted the inevitable wave of the future, with many liberals finding a more or less satisfactory blueprint in the noble experiment of Russia. The general intellectual fashion of the day was towards some sort of social utopianism.

Social Reconstruction through the schools was represented by a group of professors of education and a few professional philosophers who were orthodox followers of Deweyan progressivism save in one respect: they felt that progressive education was too objective and neutral in regard to the great social issues of the day. Perhaps the most insistent spokesman for this group was George S. Counts of Teachers College, Columbia University, whose monograph, *Dare the Schools Build a New Social Order?* set in motion the vigorous movement for indoctrination of the schools which flourished throughout the thirties and into the forties. Other advocates of the movement were Harold Rugg, John L. Childs, Goodwin Watson, Sidney Hook, Norman Woelfel, Jesse H. Newlon, and to a lesser extent, William H. Kilpatrick. An outstanding tenet of the group was the then popular one that all our social ills have an economic base so that if justice is to be achieved the economic system must be made over, by coercion if necessary. This idea was stated by Kilpatrick:

> A fundamental remaking of our economic system seems necessary so that men shall no longer be compelled to work against each other but may rather be permitted and encouraged—and if a recalcitrant minority requires it, be compelled—to cooperate for the common good.[1]

If one wants depressing evidence of what educational leaders in influential positions thought fifteen and twenty years ago I recommend a reading of the old files of the magazines *Social Frontier* and *Progressive Education;* frightened into panic by the depression, these "social thinkers" (and unfortunately, guides to budding teachers) became advocates of the class struggle, were ready to curtail freedom of the press, slant their teaching, and take care of "recalcitrant minorities." They consistently flirted with communism and looked hopefully towards Russia; Counts felt that despite the restriction of individual freedom there existed in the Soviet Union "an idealism and a driving passion for human betterment which

---

1. "The Essentials of the Activity Movement," *Progressive Education,* October, 1934.

contrast strangely with the widespread cynicism of the United States";[2] and Goodwin Watson, after a tour of Russia, decided that he had seen "a society directed toward the sustenance of major human values."[3]

It is perhaps not quite cricket to rake up the twenty-year-old mistakes of some of our educational leaders, although being reminded of them may possibly aid us in evaluating the advice and admonitions which most of them continue to offer to the public. At least two of those named above—Counts and Sidney Hook—have long since learned the bitter lesson that communism is not just a more radical liberalism but is actually a conspiracy against the whole non-Soviet world, and have both become effective anticommunist fighters. But along with the rest of this early group they retain unabated a faith in social utopianism, a utopia which is now going to be achieved not by the rough brutality of communism but by nice, democratic, Norman Thomas-ish methods.

But whatever has happened to its early disciples, Social Reconstruction in education is still with us. It is considerably less fashionable than it used to be and its advocates are no longer inclined to indulge in frank evangelizing in the open marketplace, but it is far from being moribund. I find the theory and philosophy of reconstructionism presented most fully in two rather ponderous textbooks—part of a series called the "New-World Education Series"—which are widely used in teacher training institutions. One of these, the combined labor of three professors of education, B. Othanel Smith, William O. Stanley, and J. Harlan Shores—all of the University of Illinois—is entitled *Fundamentals of Curriculum Development;* the other, by Theodore Brameld, professor of educa-

2. *The Soviet Challenge to America,* 1931, p. 330.
3. *Social Frontier,* February, 1937, p. 143.

tional philosophy at New York University, is called *Patterns of Educational Philosophy*.[4] These do not sound like something you would want to rush out and buy for bedside reading, do they? Oddly enough, you might find them, as I did, as hair-raising as a good whodunit. After a careful reading of both of them I can only say that I hope any prospective teacher who has been exposed to them will have the good sense to repudiate their message.

Messrs. Smith, Stanley, and Shores are less openly propagandistic than Professor Brameld, but although they write with a great show of scientific and sociological data and with an air of objectivity, their discussion of curriculum practices amounts to a prolonged plug for Social Reconstruction. (The authors of both these books are orthodox followers of the *methods* of progressive education but feel that its social aims are inadequate in a revolutionary age.)

In discussing the basis of the teacher's moral authority, Smith, Stanley, and Shores are quick to reject the idea that that authority might be derived from the religious tradition or any humanistic principles of the unchanging nature of man and the universe; any such "perennialism" is authoritarian and undemocratic and serves as "a bulwark of conservatism and reaction." (Query: Are Robert M. Hutchins, Mark Van Doren, and Stringfellow Barr, leading advocates of fixed principles in education, social or political conservatives?) They also turn thumbs down on the scientific method of establishing truth and authority in education; in the long run, they feel, science is as bad as religion for while it rightly refuses to accept eternal truths and subjective value judgments, some scientists in education have a tendency to try to establish ob-

4. Both published in 1950 by the World Book Company, Yonkers, New York.

jectively the dominant values in society and to devise curriculum practices that will train the student effectively in the
interests of those values. In other words, both science and religion are apt to buttress the *status quo* which is something
our authors speak of only contemptuously throughout their
book. They seem to think of the teacher as being in a perpetual
class struggle with the society in which he finds himself.
They say: "If a teacher were to succeed in his efforts to be
neutral, the effects of his success would be to strengthen the
status quo. To take no side is, in effect, to throw weight to the
side of those currently in power."[5]

If religion and science are both inadequate as the basis of
the teacher's moral authority in a period of "rapid social
change" and "cultural upset and reintegration," where shall
we look for that authority? According to the authors it comes
from "the democratic tradition." We need not be concerned
here with what, precisely, they mean by the democratic tradition or with the question of whether it is really the source of
the teacher's authority; what is instructive is to see what de-
votees of democracy and democratic principles are capable
of advocating.

They use the term "social deviate" in speaking of those
(such as criminals, alcoholics, juvenile delinquents, etc.)
whose behavior is socially unacceptable but they also feel
that a lot of people who pass for normal are deviates, or more
politely, "out of step with cultural reality," and suggest that
among these are those who believe in the free enterprise system, those who have reservations about "the assimilation of
national rights into a world order," and those who have their
fingers crossed about the ability of "refined social knowledge

---

5. Smith, Stanley, Shores, p. 386.

and insight" to regulate and integrate "basic social processes." Something has to be done about these deviates and they suggest that one of the primary tasks of curriculum development "is to build a program in which everyone can learn, through the processes of re-education, to become the kind of person demanded by the cultural patterns and realities now in the making."[6]

They reiterate the necessity for brain-washing when they point out that it is not sufficient for the curriculum to deal objectively with current affairs for this is merely being up-to-date; the criterion of Social Reconstruction "makes the school a positive force in social change and requires that the subject matter relate not only to social problems but also to collective social goals. The criterion requires, among other things, that the instructional program focus upon the reconstruction of beliefs and social norms."[7]

Nowhere do they face up to the problem of what to do with those recalcitrant parents who don't like the "cultural patterns and realities now in the making," those short-sighted parents who don't want their childrens' beliefs and social norms reconstructed; but they do speak of the duty of the educator to oppose and resist "the partial and temporary opinions of local citizens when they adversely affect the work of the public school," and of his duty to appeal "from the arbitrary decision of a particular government or of a particular locality to the mature judgment of the national community."[8] What these nebulous remarks mean is anybody's guess; mine would be that they mean that any group of parents or any local school system opposed to the tenets of modern educa-

6. *Ibid.*, pp. 114–22.
7. *Ibid.*, p. 284.
8. *Ibid.*, p. 152.

tion, including Social Reconstruction, is wrong because it is out of step with the majority of the professors of education, the National Education Association, the U.S. Office of Education, and the rest of the controlling combine of educationists.

One might suppose that it would be difficult to use more or less objective subject matter as a means of reconstructing beliefs but the authors are prepared for this objection with a frank appeal for slanting in teaching:

> There is no good reason to suppose that the content of history, English, or even mathematics could not be selected and taught in such a way as to help students to rebuild social values as well as fundamental ideas, beliefs, aspirations, skills, and methods of thinking. In this event, however, questions of "what should be" must be emphasized as much as the accumulation of factual knowledge or the development of skills.[9]

In regard to the subject of history, which can sometimes be stubbornly factual, this is what they have to say:

> Before the study of history can be justified by the criterion of democratic ideals, we must know just what aspect of historical knowledge is to be stressed, and just how this knowledge will function in human behavior as men move forward toward a fuller realization of democratic goals.[10]

A reasonably intelligent, or merely clever, history teacher who wants to "reconstruct" his pupils will have little difficulty in knowing what historical knowledge to stress and what to suppress, but surely the teacher of such neutral subjects as biology and chemistry may not find it so easy to use these subjects in rebuilding social values or changing fundamental

9. *Ibid.*, p. 387.
10. *Ibid.*, p. 265.

ideas and beliefs. But, no, the authors assure us it *is* possible to slant science teaching as well as history teaching. After making the dubious point that the questions now selected for scientific study reflect the preferences of dominant economic and social groups, such as those that control industry and agriculture (as though scientific study in these fields didn't benefit all groups) they state:

> Moreover, it seems clear, for instance, that the content of biology courses, selected by the criterion of social reconstruction in the interest of realizing the National Resources Planning Board's list of human rights, would differ radically from the content selected by the criterion of "significance to a field of organized knowledge."[11]

In other words, just as there was Nazi history and biology and there is today Soviet history and biology, we are now to have democratic history and biology—in the interests of reconstruction. (Incidentally, the "rights" promulgated by the National Resources Planning Board, as quoted by the authors, include not only the usual "right" to work, security, medical care, and so forth, but—believe it or not—the right to *rest, recreation and adventure.* This suggests a picture of citizens of the future complaining to the Ministry of Joy that despite their guaranteed right, they had had no fun this month.)

Even when the authors are not propagandizing some of their observations are of a highly conjectural nature, especially some of their sociological dicta. Attempting to prove that urban families no longer have the capacity to build "a common social perspective," they paint a melancholy picture of a family where the father leaves home early in the morning and returns in the evening, often tired and irritated from the

---

11. *Ibid.,* pp. 295–96.

troubles of the day's work, only to find that as the family gathers around the dinner table everybody else is cross, too, from the day's activities or from "the pressure of activities anticipated for the evening." This may all be true (although that does seem like an excessively petulant family) but it is hardly revolutionary. For one thing, didn't Father always go to work and haven't the authors heard that he's working shorter hours now and is around the house considerably more than he used to be? I may be unfairly attributing motives to the authors which they do not have but I suspect that their answer to the supposed disintegration of the family would be the current one that the schools must take over the functions formerly performed by the family.

The professors are aware of the difficulties of building a new curriculum which will be effective in meeting their purpose of using the schools for reconstructing society but they are not without optimism:

> Fortunately, it is not necessary to start from scratch in the development of a rationale of educational engineering. During the last twenty years a considerable amount of knowledge has been accumulated respecting the problem of *inducing and controlling changes in human relations and in the structure of social institutions.* It has been developed from sociological studies, psychological investigations of social structures and forces, research in industrial relations, public opinion surveys, and practical curriculum work. It is now possible, on the basis of this knowledge, to sketch the bold outlines of social engineering as it is applied to public education with special reference to curriculum development.[12] [Italics mine.]

If these authors give you the willies, Professor Theodore Brameld is apt to give you nightmares. His book, *Patterns of*

12. *Ibid.,* pp. 633–34.

Educational Philosophy, examines at length four philosophies of education which he calls progressivism, essentialism, perennialism, and reconstructionism; although he is sympathetic to the techniques of the first-named he thinks its social philosophy is too compromising and cautious—and the social philosophy of essentialism and perennialism he dismisses as reactionary. He is an unusually open and frank advocate of a reconstructionism which aims, as one of his critics has stated, "to establish a collectivist society which will equitably satisfy all human needs" and in the coming struggle for this society he as a reconstructionist "intends to use education as his major weapon."[13]

Brameld, like his fellow reconstructionists, Smith, Stanley, and Shores, is a great believer in democracy; indeed, the subtitle of his book is "A Democratic Interpretation," but one soon gathers that his use of the terms democracy and democratic is eccentric and that some of the things he advocates might be called by other, perhaps uglier, names. In the name of democracy, Mr. Brameld believes in what he calls "consensus" as a principle of truth-seeking; he says that "the truth of those experiences most vital in the social life of any culture" is determined by "the extent to which they are *agreed upon* by the largest possible number of the group concerned." Without this factor of consensus, he says, the experience simply is not "true."[14]

This would seem to be a twist on the pragmatic theory that "true value" is what works out satisfactorily and beneficently; Brameld says truth corresponds to what the majority wants. But the reconstructionist is obviously not satisfied with what

---

13. Frederic Lilge, "Reason and Ideology in Education," *The Harvard Educational Review*, Fall 1952, pp. 247–56.
14. Brameld, *Patterns of Educational Philosophy*, p. 456.

the majority wants as of today; it could be shown that the majority of Americans want things the reconstructionist disapproves of such as, let us say, a free economy. Here is where the reconstructionist steps in to use the school as a device for reconstructing old beliefs in a direction acceptable to the reconstructionist. In other words, he is all for what the majority wants after he has had the opportunity to mold the majority's desires.

What happens to the individual under the reconstructionist's scheme of things is explained candidly by Mr. Brameld— he gets merged into the "group mind." For the individual to function intelligently as an individual is not enough; "there is required, in addition, a revitalized 'group mind' functioning as both end and means. . . . Discipline . . . becomes the agreed-upon acceptance of orderly procedures through which groups unite in systematic efforts to articulate and to attain their goals. . . . [The minority], while free to advocate, to criticize, and to persuade if possible, is required to accept whatever rules are deemed necessary to and established for group solidarity and accomplishment."[15]

Mr. Brameld is not one to leave ideas "unarticulated," or dangling, in a vague fashion—he tells us what are some of the rules which will be deemed necessary in our reconstructed

---

15. *Ibid.*, pp. 643–44. Another professor of education sympathetic to reconstructionism, Kenneth D. Benne of Boston University, leaves us in no doubt as to who has primacy, the individual or the collective: "That a wise social policy will establish areas of privacy for persons and voluntary associations within the society is undoubtedly true. In such areas private judgment may rule. But the determination of the proper boundaries of these areas must, in an interdependent society, be based on a collective judgment." *Progressive Education*, May, 1949.

society. For instance, if indoctrination is to be successful, children must go to school much earlier than they do now:

> Where *both* parents assume some form of out-of-the-home responsibility (as we should expect the vast majority to do with the coming of the new society), attendance of children after the first twelve months is expected for two or more hours daily, depending upon parental schedules and home supervision.
>
> Where the mother remains full-time with her children (believing that she is thus realizing herself fully) attendance is optional until the age of about three and one-half years; while from that age until six the average child must attend a minimum of three hours daily. The assumption here is that a combination of home and school experience for very small children is desirable—that, while the mother's care is ordinarily needed also, this should be supplemented by expert guidance in habit-formation, for example, during these crucially formative years.[16]

Mr. Brameld believes that in a collectivist society education cannot be left to the whims of private individuals or local communities. He advocates the formation of a Federal Education Authority which would be charged with carrying out the following *minimum* blueprint:

> An educational system (a) supported heavily by federal taxation, supplemented by local resources, and controlled by the service state; (b) offering completely free universal education from the nursery school through the university and adult levels; (c) gearing curriculums, teaching, guidance, and administration to the purposes of the economy of abundance, service state, scientific society, and esthetic order; (d) bringing newspapers, radio chains, and other instruments of public enlightenment into direct cooperation with education and under similar controls.[17]

16. *Ibid.*, pp. 610–11.
17. *Ibid.*, p. 662.

Mr. Brameld has a lot of other "future-centered goals" for our "culture-in-crisis," goals which he says only the radically democratic minority now support but which it is the duty of the schools to sell to the majority. It is a long list and if you want to read it I refer you to pages 498, 499, and 500 in his book but here is a partial list of some of the things he thinks the schools ought to be advocating: guaranteed income for all, sufficient to meet expertly determined standards of shelter, dress, medical care, education, and recreation; nationalization of all natural resources and enterprises of monopolistic tendency; subsidization of scientists and artists; not only complete security for old people but "rich companionship"; tax-supported music, movies, drama, and painting; a world democracy dedicated to applying all these "principles" on an international scale.

This seems like a large order but on the whole Professor Brameld is optimistic, even enthusiastic, about the possibilities of the school's role in such an ambitious program. (At one point, it is true, he expresses some discouragement with liberal democracy's vacillation and uncertainty, and then asks: "Should it not be contrasted with the social devotion, loyalty, and purposefulness which millions of young citizens elsewhere in the world seem now to be acquiring, and which serve as bulwarks of strength to their countries?" Now I wonder what young citizens in what countries he could be referring to here?[18]) Along with Smith, Stanley, and Shores he

---

18. *Ibid.*, p. 559. Another educator who is not a reconstructionist but a distinguished representative of the liberal arts at Harvard University, has been more specific about who these young citizens are: "The calm good faith of the younger Russian generation in each other and in their culture is in contrast to the uneasiness evident in the American world lest personal relations, business

seems to feel that we are developing a "rationale of educational engineering" and that we are rapidly learning how to "induce" and "control" changes in people and institutions. As a matter of fact, in this regard Mr. Brameld is no ivory tower theorist but has himself done some educational engineering in a real school situation and has given us a report of the results in an earlier book called *Design for America*.[19] Perhaps it will be worth considering for a moment as one example of how a reconstructionist actually went about the task of indoctrinating real students in a real school.

During the year 1944 Mr. Brameld (then an associate professor at the University of Minnesota) conducted an experiment with the junior and senior students at the Fleetwood High School, Floodwood, Minnesota, an experiment described in *Design for America*. The object of the experimenter was to find out what conclusions young people would come to if they devoted some time to the discussion of the theme, What kind of society do we want for the future? For over four months these sixteen and seventeen year olds devoted two hours each school day to "[building] by cooperative thinking and exploration a blueprint of our future society."[20] As far as classroom procedure was concerned, this consisted mostly of discussion of large general economic, political, scientific, social, and educational problems and propositions, such as civil liberties, federal subsidization of art and science, race equality, city planning, TVA, socialized medicine, etc.

---

relations, labor relations, or any other of a dozen connections between individual and individual shall prove deceptive." Howard Mumford Jones, *Education and World Tragedy* (Cambridge; Harvard University Press, 1946), pp. 105–106.

19. Theodore Brameld, *Design for America* (New York; Hinds, Hayden & Eldredge, Inc., 1945).

20. *Ibid.*, p. 3.

It is of interest to observe the manner in which this experiment was conducted by Professor Brameld and his associates, a manner inevitable if your aim educationally is to indoctrinate. It is quite plain, after reading over the statement of objectives, the suggested syllabi, and the examination questions, that those who conducted the experiment were not interested solely in a healthy discussion of controversial issues but were trying deliberately to convert students to the idea that the traditional, relatively uncontrolled, American economic and political system needs to be scrapped in favor of a collectivist system. To discover how successful their methods were, the experimenters gave at the beginning and the end of the project an Attitudes Test which consisted of ninety-six statements which the student was either to affirm or deny, the purpose of the test being to determine if the student had made "any real gain in the direction of liberality of thought." "The experts who keyed the test" (experts in liberality, apparently) were the five individuals who conducted the experiment.

One has almost to admire the effrontery of these five in deciding what is the "correct" attitude for young students to have on a wide variety of complex, controversial social matters. If the student denied that the following statements, among others, were true he was marked down as being "illiberal":

If European countries want to establish left-wing governments after the war, we should support them.

What this country needs is more T.V.A.'s.

The federal government should finance government projects for the advancement of the arts.

Income taxes on the rich should be greatly increased.

Wealth should be much more equally distributed.

The government should take over much larger areas of northern Minnesota iron mines now entirely in private hands.

Our economic base must be shifted from rugged individualism to economic planning.

The student was also considered to lack liberality of thought if he felt the following statements were true:

Liberal interpretation of the Constitution has permitted too great expansion of the powers of the federal government.

A program of public works should be instituted after the war only if widespread unemployment returns.

Public education ought not to be supported by federal funds.

Any American can climb to success if he has the will.

There is too much bureaucracy in government already.

Free competition is essential to healthy operation of our economic system in normal times.

The more state authority and the less federal authority, the better.

Without individual competition for profits, our economy would slow up and soften.[21]

The test, of course, established nothing about the students' liberality, or lack of it, but it did establish that those in charge had a definite set of socio-economic values about which they felt so strongly they wished to indoctrinate the students under their care. (Building up "consensus" is what I suppose the reconstructionist would say he was doing.) This indoctrination was of public school students, many of whose parents undoubtedly held different social, political, and economic values than those of the experimenters and certainly were not paying taxes and sending their children to school for the purpose of having those values undermined. I am all in favor of discussing controversial political and social questions in

21. *Ibid.*, pp. 144–50.

the classroom and I cannot see how the teacher in introducing such questions can suppress his own opinions or why he should; but any discriminating teacher knows the difference between declaring his own opinion and proselytizing. It is impossible to accept Mr. Brameld's assurance that this was an objective scientific experiment or the claim that it was carried on in a democratic manner and aimed to promote an understanding of democracy. If having students spend five months discussing a "design for America" when their instructors had the design neatly drawn up in advance is an "experiment in democracy" then the term democracy is being used in the Orwellian New Speak sense.

The reader may be relieved to know that the experimenters were not altogether encouraged by the response to the Attitudes Test. They reported that the results at the end of the experiment showed that "while there was an increase in definiteness of conviction, there is no marked assurance as to whether this definiteness was toward a 'greater liberality'— that is, a stronger and more consistent point of view harmonious with the democratic criterion developed early in the project."[22] However, one startling result of the experiment was that "a majority agreed also that socialism and communism are in the libertarian stream of political evolution, and hence more allied with than opposed to democracy."[23] It is hard to understand how a professor, even a professor of education, at one of our largest universities, could be so historically ignorant as to believe, or to let a majority of his students believe, that communism is allied to libertarianism or democracy.

Both of the textbooks I have mentioned in this chapter—

22. *Ibid.*, p. 120.
23. *Ibid.*, p. 22.

Fundamentals of Curriculum Development by Smith, Stanley, and Shores, and *Patterns of Educational Philosophy* by Professor Brameld—are used in teacher-training courses at several colleges and universities. It is hard to believe that these institutions want to turn out people who will do the kind of teaching advocated by the authors of these books. Do they actually want American public schools staffed by persons who think the teacher is engaged in a perpetual class struggle, who look upon education not as a means of improving the individual but as indoctrination for a new social order, and who believe that selected and slanted teaching of subject matter is a decent or legitimate device?

One does not for a moment challenge the right of the authors to advocate the remaking of America to conform to their prejudices or to write books to that purpose. But if they do write them they should be presented for what they are— special pleading for a cause, so the student would at least know what to expect and could evaluate it accordingly. These books are written by men who call themselves scholars and are put forward as scientific discussions of educational matters but actually the authors are zealots and reformers who are writing propaganda.

How widespread Social Reconstruction is as a conscious educational theory in our public schools is difficult to know. Messrs. Smith, Stanley, Shores, and Brameld are undoubtedly the extremists of the movement but there are echoes of reconstructionism in the utterances of many other trainers of teachers and in the pronouncements of professional educational organizations. Among the latter is the now famous statement of the American Association of School Administrators in which we are informed that as the community is "a primary and an ultimate functional entity—an end in itself" the individual must be merged in the community and a shift made in our educational system "from helping to educate the individual in his own right to become a valuable member of society, to the preparation of the individual for the realization of his best self in the higher loyalty of serving the basic ideals and aims of our society"—all of which calls, as you can well imagine, for "a vast stepping up of the functions of government on all levels."[24] If we bear in mind that this statement emanates not from some obscure group of zealots but from the leading organization of school administrators, perhaps we have some indication of how influential reconstructionism is in the public schools.

We must certainly acknowledge that the course of history for the first fifty years of the twentieth century has been on the side of the reconstructionists; these have been the years when security and conformity have become the goal of millions, when the traditional liberal ideal of the widest possible freedom for the exercise of individual energy has steadily lost ground. If that ideal should have a recrudescence in the second half of the century—and some optimists profess to see faint signs of life—we can expect the philosophy of reconstructionism to gradually wither. As this recrudescence is as yet only a pious hope, believers in freedom ought not to miss any opportunities for pointing out that reconstructionism in education is essentially a scheme for the manipulation of man, and can only function successfully through the employment of totalitarian political methods.

Reconstructionism is probably a good deal easier to combat

---

24. *Schools for a New World,* Twenty-Fifth Yearbook, American Association of School Administrators (Washington, D.C., 1947), pp. 43, 44.

than Life Adjustment for its tenets and the coercive methods essential to their fulfillment are probably still repugnant to a large body of Americans. But the superficial attractions of Life Adjustment give it a much more seductive appeal: who would oppose adjusting students to their environment and teaching them how to get along with other people and how to be personally attractive, and all the rest of it? Those who believe that the cultivation of intelligence is not an easy task but that it must be a primary part of the work of the school, those who believe that a developed intelligence can adapt itself to all life situations—these advocates of intelligence are going to have a hard time trying to convince the converts to Life Adjustment that the easy, seductive way only leads down the garden path.

American public school education will only throw off the incubus of these two false philosophies by restoring the centrality of the individual in education. We must adopt again the idea that the purpose of education is the improvement of the individual and when we achieve this we can be assured that the quality of the group will rise and society will be sounder.

V

The Stranglehold of the Educationists

Many of the troubles which beset public education are directly traceable to an etymological phenomenon which has engaged the attention of a host of critics in recent years but does not yet seem to be comprehended by the general lay public: the transfiguration of the word education into Education, an event that first became visible to the naked eye about fifty years ago, was then no bigger than a man's hand, and has now mushroomed into a cloud which envelops our whole educational system. My 1934 edition of Webster's Collegiate Dictionary defines education as "the act or process of education; the impartation or acquisition of knowledge, skill, or development of character, as by study or discipline"; it also refers to education as "pedagogics." The 1951 edition of the same dictionary, while retaining the first part of this definition, has elevated the pedagogics part to "a science dealing with the principles and practice of teaching and learning." In the process of becoming a science, of acquiring a capital E, education has enhanced its position as a field of study; as the act or process of imparting knowledge it has steadily lost ground. And as the art of pedagogics has developed into the science of education, it has also become a vested interest, supported by a gigantic interlocking bureaucracy which controls public education and is beginning to threaten private education.

Some historians trace the germination of this monstrous growth to some innocent remarks made by President James B. Angell of the University of Michigan to his Board of Regents in 1874. As many graduates of that university went into public school work, he thought that "some familiar lectures" on "the art of teaching and governing a school" might be of "essential service" to the senior class.[1] Four years later Michigan established a chair of "the Science and the Art of Teaching" (apparently the first such chair in this country) but the idea was slow to catch on: twenty years later, in 1900, only about a dozen colleges and universities had established chairs of pedagogy or departments of education. But by 1954 practically every self-respecting university in the country (Princeton is a notable exception) had a booming department of education, with the aim no longer being as simple a one as providing "some familiar lectures on the art of teaching and governing a school." President Angell's modest suggestion was prompted by the realization of a need that is as real now as it was in his day, the teacher's need not only for knowledge of subject matter but for craftsmanship in presenting it and for knowledge of the nature of the recipient of subject matter, the child. I imagine there are very few die-hards who would maintain that all true teachers are born, not made, that thorough knowledge of one's subject automatically equips one to teach it brilliantly or who would deny that some aspects of the art of teaching can be transmitted. But today the art has become more important than the matter, the method has

---

1. Knight, *Fifty Years of American Education,* p. 231.

taken precedence over the material it was called into being to serve.

Had it not been for one circumstance pedagogics might have remained a relatively minor part of the preparation of teachers and would have continued to be taught by subject matter authorities, with history specialists giving sideline lectures on how to teach history, mathematics professors doing the same for their subject, and so on through the whole field of the liberal arts. But along about the turn of the century education began to be affected by the influence of the new philosophy of pragmatism which was marked, as Santayana observed, by "the dominance of the foreground," by excessive concern with method, with *how* rather than *why*. Of the triumvirate who fathered pragmatism—Charles Peirce, William James, and John Dewey—it was the latter who related it to education; his pioneering book, *The School and Society*, and subsequent books of his, were challenging, indeed revolutionary, for they called into question many of the presumptions on which the older, traditional education was based, especially the education of the very young. Dewey attracted followers and disciples (many of them, as has often been pointed out, far more extreme than the master) and between them they formulated certain philosophical and pedagogical principles which formed the basis of what came to be known as progressive education and is now more commonly referred to as modern education. I do not think anyone will challenge the statement that pragmatism has become the official philosophy of public school education; there may be an occasional maverick scattered here and there but the great majority of the professors of education are committed to this philosophy and they transmit it to the future teachers and administrators whom they train to run the American public school system.[2]

The intricacies of pragmatism do not unravel themselves easily to the amateur in philosophy, especially as set down in the somewhat involuted prose of Professor Dewey, but looming out of the misty and obscure lowlands are discernible certain mountain peaks of meaning for educational philosophy and practice. In some respects the educational conservative and the educational pragmatist can meet on common ground: both believe in the concept of humaneness, that is, that children should be treated with kindness, that cuffing them around and smacking them over the knuckles with rulers is not a sure-fire method of imparting knowledge; the traditionalist can agree that the child needs to live a happy and creative life in the present as well as in some remote future; and he would agree that education in the past often failed to recognize the value of action, the attempt to relate thinking and doing, the mental and the physical, the idea summed up by a nonpragmatist, Jacques Maritain, in the remark that man's intelligence is not only in his head but in his fingers. But beyond these agreements there is a wide gulf separating traditionalist and pragmatist, especially the contemporary pragmatist who in practice often goes beyond anything dreamed of by the founding fathers of the movement.

The pragmatist, following the lead of Dewey, is reluctant to postulate any ultimate values toward which the educational process ought to be aiming, to set up any ends for education;

2. There were, and still are, well-known figures in professional education opposed to much that goes by the names of pragmatism and progressivism. Several names come to mind: William C. Bagley, Frederick S. Breed, Ross L. Finney, I. L. Kandel, Edgar W. Knight, Robert Ulich. These men, however, are the lonely exceptions.

to him the educational process has no end beyond itself. Education is "the reconstruction of experience," it is continued growth. While the concept of growth is central to the pragmatist's position, he is careful to avoid any statement about what direction it should take, except that he sometimes speaks vaguely of "desirable" and "satisfactory" growth; to go beyond this would be to commit oneself to some ultimate values, to absolutes, and this is something the pragmatist refuses to do even though here he runs into a logical absurdity: if you declare something to be desirable and satisfactory you are implying an *ought to be*, you are declaring that there *are* some desirable ends.

What are the implications of this viewpoint for what goes on in classrooms? If, as the pragmatist maintains, the important thing is the "on-going process" rather than any results obtained, curriculum makers will not acknowledge any hierarchy of values among subjects; no subject will be of any more intrinsic value than any other; courses in pastry-making and basket-weaving will be on a par with courses in history and literature. In the pragmatist's world the important criterion in education is usefulness; the schools should be providing the student with experiences which will contribute in concrete fashion to "successful living" now and in the future. The curriculum will be determined not by any preconceived notion of what is important for all students but by what appeals to the interests, and is compatible with the abilities, of individual students. Effective learning is not something gleaned from books or from contemplation of the dead past but is learning by doing, by re-creating "real-life experiences" in the classroom. The task of schools and teachers must not be the narrowly intellectual one of inculcating knowledge, of transmitting the cultural heritage; it must be nothing less than the attempt to meet the needs of the whole child, not only the intellectual needs, but the emotional, recreational, social, and all other needs. Although the pragmatist often speaks of the ethical and spiritual needs of youth and how they can be met in school, his rejection of transcendental values causes him to think of them solely in secular and social terms; in his lexicon, the ethical and spiritual way becomes an exercise in cooperative living, in how-to-get-along-with-each-other.

In previous chapters I have indirectly touched on the inadequacies of the pragmatic position as a guide to sound educational practice. For emphasis, I will elaborate briefly on some of those objections. The primary objection is to pragmatism's lack of a value-system, its lack of a sense of direction. That is "true value," the pragmatist asserts, which "works out" beneficently in social fruits, but if we deny that there is an ultimate truth which sometimes transcends time and fact, if we have no absolute standard of what is good and what bad, how are we to judge what is "beneficent"? Won't our answer be determined by our social and cultural conditioning, so that if we are Russians we will decide that communism is beneficent and democracy evil? There are many pragmatists, of course, who do operate as if there were for them ultimate values and who do make moral discriminations but one feels they do this despite their philosophy. It is hard to escape the conclusion of the philosopher Eliseo Vivas: "No Deweyan can give one good, radically theoretical reason, one that goes beyond expedience, why he prefers democracy to totalitarianism or why he regards other men as his moral equals."[3]

3. *The Moral Life and the Ethical Life* (Chicago; University of Chicago Press, 1950), p. 128.

Nor is the pragmatist's definition of education as continued growth—Dewey's "experiential continuum"—satisfactory until we set up some goals for growth; one can grow and develop in evil, one can graduate from efficiency at petty thievery to efficiency in murder. Another unsatisfactory criterion is usefulness: who can say what is useful and what isn't? How are we to tell that what seems useless at the moment may not bear unpredictable future fruit, as the young Churchill's painful exposure to grammar and rhetoric bore fruit in his later literary and political career? And if the student gets pleasure from pursuing some obscure aspect of a subject, is that to be dismissed as useless?

I think the pragmatist-schoolman's preoccupation with "real-life experiences" can also be misleading, especially when it fails to take into sufficient consideration the fact that children are not only attracted by the comfortably familiar but by the unfamiliar and the strange, in short, that they are still, despite all the educators have done to undermine them, creatures of imagination and fantasy. When the schoolman agrees with the remark of the American sociologist who intimates that city children can't understand the sentiment in "I remember, I remember the house where I was born" or "over the river and through the wood to grandfather's house we'll go" because they were born in hospitals and spend their holidays in movie palaces,[4] isn't he agreeing that children only appreciate what they know and have no sense of imagination or capacity for vicarious enjoyment? And isn't it comforting to know that this is not so, even in the sociologist's and the schoolman's fast changing world?

4. Margaret Mead, *The School in American Culture* (Cambridge; Harvard University Press, 1951), pp. 25-26.

I am willing to accept the pragmatist's statement that the curriculum must be based on the child's interests and abilities as a partially valid doctrine; it is uncontestably true that all students do not have the same interests or abilities and that learning will be most effective when these differences are recognized. I am unwilling to accept the current version of this doctrine which is used as justification for the notion that those who (seemingly) lack interest or ability need not be educated but merely adjusted. Nor do I find it easy to accept the companion doctrine that the school must educate the whole child; to do so it would have to assume the functions of the home and community, to the neglect of its own functions.

The traditionalist-humanist asserts that men must be bound together by ties of moral stability and he considers that true education for all men will consist of studies that illumine and strengthen those ties. The educational pragmatist, on the other hand, lacking belief in man's need for such a central moral stability, sees no necessity for a common education which will connect man with man and man with nature. But without this belief in a common bond between man and man education tends to become animal training, with the educator occupying himself more and more in a search for refined *method;* the *content* of education—those studies appropriate to all men— tends to get submerged by the empirical and the "practical," by fragments of information and skills.

It is said that philosophy has no appeal for the average, practical mind, especially the average, practical American mind. When Albert Lynd made the reasonable prediction that the majority of parents would vote against Deweyan prag- matism "if they understood the philosophical ballot" one edu- cationist replied that parents aren't interested in philosophy but are satisfied if the new education "works."[5] Another educationist refers to "superficial critics" of the schools "with their remote philosophical arguments," and says that "the whole conflict over relative and absolute values is a tempest in a teapot as it applies to the process of education."[6] This cavalier dismissal of philosophical conflict reminds one of John Maynard Keynes' remark that practical men, who believe themselves to be exempt from any intellectual influences, are usually the slaves of some academic scribbler of a few years back. No matter how much educators scoff at philosophy for the masses, or fail to see the philosophical basis of their own actions, the fact remains that conditions in our public schools today stem from a philosophy, from a way of looking at man and the universe; and if we would understand why conditions are what they are we will need to understand the philosophy.

As I have pointed out, the progress of education as Education was slow until about 1900 when the theories of Dewey and his disciples began to be felt. The pragmatists took over public education by following their own precepts; as Dean Marten Ten Hoor has pointed out, they emphasized *pragma,* the *deed,* the *thing done.* These early pragmatists in the colleges were men of action, not content to idle in academic backwaters as were the scholars on the liberal arts faculties. Convinced of the great importance of the *how* of things, of methodology, they proceeded rapidly in the nurture of Professional Education, that infant which has now grown into such

5. See "Who Wants Progressive Education?" by Albert Lynd, *Atlantic Monthly,* April, 1953, and the reply thereto in the May, 1953, issue of the same magazine, "How Dangerous is John Dewey?" by Frederic Ernst.
6. Ernest O. Melby, "And the Future of School Administration?" *The School Executive,* January, 1954.

an over-sized adult. The progress of this nurture is well described by Dean Ten Hoor:

> The leaders convinced university administrators. They "sold" the school of education to the students and to the public. They organized teacher employment offices on university campuses and refused to recommend students who had not had the requisite number and kind of courses in education and they were thus able to fill the field with their own graduates. They joined forces with teachers colleges and normal schools and built up a great, state-wide organization of teachers, principals and superintendents, each of whom was a partisan in his own community. They convinced the public and the state legislatures of the rightness of their cause. They gained virtual control of the laws and the administration of teacher certification. They became a powerful, sometimes a dominating, influence in accrediting associations in the field of higher education. They established their own type of high school curricula and compelled many colleges and universities to alter their admission requirements and even their requirements for graduation. In short . . . the schoolmen acquired control of publicly supported primary and secondary education in the United States, and, as a consequence, considerable influence over the course of private education on these levels.[7]

As the schools of education and the teachers colleges have now become the dominant force in public education by controlling teacher-preparation, it might be well to look a little more closely at their influence. Many parents and laymen, I find, do not seem to realize how a teacher qualifies for a position in our public schools today. Once upon a time bright young girls and boys who did good work in college could go immediately into public school teaching; if they wanted to

---

7. "The Stake of the Liberal Arts College in Teacher Certification," *Association of American Colleges Bulletin,* March, 1953.

teach in high school they probably took advanced or post-graduate work in the subject they wanted to teach. Such a preparation no longer qualifies one to teach in public schools; many of these bright young people now go into private school teaching where the salaries are no greater and the hours on duty no shorter but where there is usually some respect for learning and scholarship. A sound education and a knowledge of one's subject is no longer the prime qualification for getting into public school teaching; the modern emphasis on *how* rather than *what* dictates that the prospective teacher must spend about one-fourth of the period of his higher education taking courses in Education; moreover, if he attends a teachers college his work in the traditional subjects will probably be directed not by experts in these subjects but experts in how to teach them.

Preoccupation with methodology and pedagogical gadgetry is certainly not entirely useless. Probably Stephen Leacock was close to the truth of the matter when he described Education as consisting of "10 per cent solid value and 90 per cent mixed humbug and wind." A knowledge of the history of education, of the psychology of learning and growth, and some hours in practice teaching are important in the training of all teachers, but those responsible for teacher training are not content with anything so modest in the way of professional preparation.

Under an ideal system, prospective teachers in their student days would come under the tutelage of the best scholars and authorities in various subject fields. But these scholars, who *do* influence the training of those who are going to teach in private schools or in liberal arts colleges, have practically no effect on the training of public school teachers. By the educators they are often looked upon as old fuddy-duddies, poking around in the trash basket of the stuffy past. The great dichotomy in American education today is between the world of scholarship and learning on the one hand, and on the other, the world of educational *Realpolitik* dominated by the schools of education in our universities, the teachers colleges, the National Education Association and its subsidiaries, the U.S. Office of Education, and the state departments of education, all working together with great unanimity of purpose as the gigantic pressure group which controls public education.

The chief method the Education lobby has used to gain control has been through the certification of teachers; they have so effectively lobbied their point of view in the state legislatures that today only a miracle can get a well-qualified person in the scholastic sense into the schools without exposure to "professional" education. Superintendents, who almost invariably are themselves products of the teacher-training schools, sell their boards the idea that only those teachers should be advanced in the system who go back to the schools of education for periodic doses of indoctrination. (Encouraged by their easy successes of recent years, educators are now lobbying to make "professional" requirements mandatory for teaching in private schools and colleges.)

There is increasing evidence to show that the teacher-training institutions—which have, in the words of the Harvard Report, "taught everything except the indispensible thing, the love of knowledge"—are providing us with teachers who are our most poorly educated citizens. In 1927 Nicholas Murray Butler said that teachers in the United States were "in large part quite uneducated in any large and justifiable sense of that word"; in 1937 William C. Bagley of Teachers College said that of all comparable countries, "the United States may have the least well-selected and least well-educated teachers"; in 1938 Learned and Wood, in a study of conditions in Pennsylvania, said that the teachers in training, compared with the nonteachers, exhibited inferiority in "nearly every department of study."[8] That conditions have not improved since these pessimistic statements were made, is shown by the depressing evidence to be found in the results of the draft deferment examinations given to over 300,000 students in 1951 in which those students majoring in education made by far the poorest showing. According to findings published by the Educational Testing Service, of 97,800 college freshmen tested those who scored highest were students of engineering, with 68 per cent passing; then came the physical sciences, 64 per cent; biological sciences, 59 per cent; social sciences, 57 per cent; the humanities, 52 per cent; general arts, 48 per cent; business, 42 per cent; agriculture, 37 per cent; and then, at the end of the procession, education with only 27 per cent. According to the report, seniors in education who took the test did about the same as the freshmen. And from these men we are to draw the future leaders and administrators of our public school system![9]

Many teachers, of course, are not themselves happy about present conditions in the field of teacher training or about the adulteration of real education. Any publicist, lay or schoolman, who touches on these subjects in print is apt to hear immediately from a host of teachers who are only too happy to find a sympathetic ear in which to pour their woes. (Many of them request that their names not be used, for fear of reprisals from their educator bosses.) The gist of their com-

8. Knight, *op. cit.*, pp. 279–81.
9. Henry Chauncy, "The Use of the Selective Service College Qualification Test in the Deferment of College Students," *Science*, July 25, 1952.

plaints is that their training, and supervision after they become teachers, is of a kind to discourage any realistic and fundamental approach to the problem of educating, rather than merely chaperoning, the children under their charge.

It is a healthy sign that many persons both in the field of the liberal arts and of professional education, who cannot by the wildest flight of the imagination be dubbed enemies of the schools, have of late been looking critically at this question of teacher preparation. Harold L. Clapp, of the division of language and literature at Grinnell College, in a trenchant article titled "The Stranglehold on Education," says:

> No dyed-in-the-wool Educationist really seems to believe that knowledge of a subject has much to do with teaching that subject. Subject-matter requirements for teachers are pitifully inadequate, and cannot well be otherwise. There is much too little time to study the *subject* one is to teach when so much time is taken up by courses in *how* to teach. . . .
>
> The appalling fact is that *our most poorly educated college graduates are our teachers.* [Author's italics.] A college which would raise its academic standards is invariably hindered by the plight of the prospective teacher, who because of "professional" requirements cannot carry more than a minimum of academic work. There are reputable colleges in the United States which have established the requirements for their A.B. degree at a high level, but which make a specific exception of the teacher-in-training. While they phrase it less baldly, their catalogues state in effect: "If you are going to be *educated* while in college, you must do this, and this, and this. If you are going to *teach instead,* less is expected of you."[10]

This is what historian Arthur E. Bestor of the University of Illinois has to say:

10. *Bulletin* of the American Association of University Professors, Summer, 1949.

American intellectual life is threatened because the first twelve years of formal schooling in the United States are falling more and more completely under the policy-making control of a new breed of educator who has no real place in—who does not respect and who is not respected by—the world of scientists, scholars, and professional men.[11]

Dean Roger P. McCutcheon of the Graduate School of Tulane University, regretting the tendency to increase Education requirements, says:

If we really want those who teach our children to have stopped their subject-matter education at the sophomore level, well and good, but we should realize it. We are now face to face with a plan that will require prospective teachers to abandon the Bachelor of Arts degree for an undergraduate degree in education. Furthermore, there is as yet no convincing proof that these education requirements make better teachers.[12]

Criticisms such as the foregoing may, in view of the fact that the critics represent the humanities, be interpreted as the cries of those who see a threat to their own vested interests. Lately, however, some pained voices have been raised from within the temple itself. Frank E. Spaulding, who is a professor of education emeritus (Yale), wrote an article a few years ago in which he deplored the widespread obeisance of superintendents of schools to the dictums of the super-professionals (his term). He feels that superintendents have permitted the super-professionals to determine what is sound preparation for teaching and for advancing in a school system; invariably such preparation means more and more exposure to courses

11. *Educational Wastelands,* p. 121.
12. "The Master's Degree and the Teacher Requirements," *School and Society,* September, 22, 1951.

in schools of education. Under the present system, he points out, the poorest teacher in more than 94 per cent of all city school systems in this country, can climb steadily from the foot to the top of the salary scale while the best teacher will remain at the foot if she chooses not to take the courses. The whole present-day setup of salary schedules, says Dr. Spaulding, "is a perfect example of the advantages of cooperation—for those who cooperate. The prosperity and to a large extent even the livelihood of the super-professionals is dependent on the maintenance of these schedules. Teachers serving under them would be foolish not to take advantage of the large salary increments which result from the hours and years devoted to 'preparation,' and to repeated doses of 'preparation,' which the super-professionals are eager to provide."

Dr. Spaulding, indeed, seems to be a thoroughly disillusioned educationist. In his opinion educators use novel and difficult language and dress up trite thought in new linguistic garments; and he complains that most of them are isolated from the schools, pointing out that of the half-dozen most widely recognized contemporary leaders among the super-professionals, three have never had any direct service in schools and the service of the others was very brief and in each case was completed over forty years ago.[13]

Edgar W. Knight, who until his death in 1953 was Kenan Professor of Educational History at the University of North Carolina, was another educator who felt that all is far from right in the world of teacher training. Complaining of the increased number of courses in education thought up by the teacher-training institutions in cahoots with the certifying bureaus and state departments of education, he said:

---

13. "Coping With Modern Educational Ideas," *Teacher Education Quarterly* (Connecticut), Spring, 1950.

In this fact friendly critics see tendencies toward what would promptly be stamped as crass and vulgar racketeering in less humane activities. It is this condition that causes students to say—generally after they have become bachelor, master, or doctor of education—that the courses they were forced to take were so overlapping and repetitious as to be almost immoral. Out of these and other unhealthy conditions that have grown up and nowadays surround practices in teacher-education, the critics see the rapid tendency for teacher-education institutions to become mere trade-schools and their products often mere mechanics.[14]

In a later article, Dr. Knight returned to the subject of proliferation and inflation of the curriculum in schools of education, stating that these conditions "enable and even encourage indifferent and sometimes quite weak students to become teachers and managers of the schools with comparatively little intellectual effort, if they but learn to give the passwords and pronounce the pedagogical shibboleths."[15]

The educationists, who are the authors of the system, refuse to believe that the poor quality of current teaching has anything to do with the kind of institutions they are running. Their argument is that we are getting poor candidates for teacher training because of the low financial returns. (There is not nearly as great a shortage of teachers in private schools as there is in public ones, even though the financial returns are no greater and often less.) While it is true, and has always been true, that one of the reasons many persons of ability will not enter the profession is that it is a notoriously underpaid

14. "The Obligation of Professional Education to the Schools," *School and Society*, October 6, 1951.

15. "Some Disturbing Educational Contradictions," *School and Society*, November 29, 1952.

one, I believe there are now more compelling deterrents. Any intelligent young person who feels strongly about education wants for himself, and if he becomes a teacher wants to transmit, the best possible sort of education, but he suspects that he is not going to get this kind of education under present teacher-training auspices. The fact seems to be that the greatest deterrent to entering the profession of public school teaching is that it has become intellectually disreputable. If the teacher-training institutions have little regard for real education, for scholastic and intellectual attainment, they will attract individuals who share this disregard—precisely the indifferent and weak students to which Dr. Knight referred. One school of education in a large university states the case frankly in its catalogue: "Students will be admitted to the college of education without reference to high school pattern, only high school education being a requirement."

Under the present scheme of things it is almost impossible for an able, scholarly, and conscientious teacher to advance in the system without pocketing his or her pride and returning to summer school for further doses of "professional preparation." This usually consists of courses in methodology, often dull, sometimes repellent; and the courses in subject matter are apt to be superficial survey courses, like the summer course in one teachers college which deals with World Literature from ancient times to the twentieth century—all in thirty days! The fashionable gimmick at the moment in professional preparation is something called the "workshop" (sometimes, to add scientific tone, called the "laboratory workshop") which is a sort of round table discussion enabling teachers to get academic credit for agreeing with the educational clichés expressed by the professional educator who presides. The *sine qua non* of these workshops is agreement; the teacher who cannot conform is guilty of the great modern sin in the eyes of educators—noncooperation with the group.

I imagine that any able teacher is going to be discouraged by the results of a recent "study" which shows that the majority of teacher-training institutions believe they must prepare teachers for "correlated, fused, broad-field, core types of curriculum organization in secondary schools." One can well believe the statement in the same report that "traditional majors and minors" will not help the teacher preparing to teach core, for a knowledge of subject matter may be only a handicap to the teacher who is trying to keep subject matter out of her teaching.[16]

The good teacher is apt to become resentful about all this foolishness and either quit teaching or become embittered and soured—while the ambitious and superficial teachers take all the snap courses, attend the workshops, and become the administrators who set the standards for teaching. Incidentally, to some aspiring candidate for an educational doctorate, seeking a subject for a thesis, I make a gratuitous suggestion: why not investigate the high incidence of physical education graduates among public school administrators and their influence on the intellectual tone of the schools. While I offer no supporting statistics, I have been surprised in travelling around the country how many superintendents of schools are drawn from this field. In one of our largest school systems the deputy superintendent in charge of curriculum is an ex-basketball coach. I don't mean to belittle physical educationists but only to point out that their training is not usually of the sort which

---

16. *Vitalizing Secondary Education, op. cit.,* p. 27.

qualifies them to set the intellectual character or course of studies of a school system.

I realize that my strictures against the teacher-training institutions may seem too sweeping to some persons, but hardly to those who know something of their character. The surprising thing is that sometimes one will find sound scholars in these institutions, men who quietly resist the nonsense served up by the rest of the staff. If anyone wants to maintain that one of the worst things that ever happened to American education was the formation of Teachers College, Columbia University, I am willing to go along with him and add that I deplore its continuing influence; the fact remains that there have been scholars at Teachers College who made great contributions to education. From my observation, the best people on the staffs of the schools of education are apt to be the professors of educational history (who are often genuine historians) and the professors of educational philosophy (who are sometimes genuine philosophers). The worst seem to be the professors of "administration" most of whom seem to qualify for their jobs by failing as superintendents of schools.

The professional educators are now bent on extending their control beyond teacher certification and seem to be attempting to make the schools entirely autonomous, to divorce them from the natural and normal workings of the political process and put them entirely under the tutelage of the experts. Chiefly through the lobbying efforts of the National Education Association, which with its numerous affiliated associations numbers almost a million in membership, efforts have been afoot for some time to erect a system under which public education is subject to less and less public control. The tendencies for state legislatures, under pressures from the education lobby, to set up provisions whereby the public school system has first call on state revenues; the increasing number of cities where school boards are elected separately from other officials; the tendency to remove all state functions of education from the jurisdiction of the governor and local functions from the jurisdiction of mayor or selectman—all of these things may, at first glance, seem like worthy objectives, as removing education from "politics." But public education, like roads and sanitary arrangements, *is* a part of the function of government, of politics; you can separate it and give it special and preferential treatment only to the detriment of the over-all governmental process. So-called independent school boards (those elected at separate elections) often turn out to be independent of other municipal or town functions but under the domination of educationists; nor are they necessarily less susceptible to political graft as witness the scandals of a year or so ago relating to members of the Los Angeles board of education.[17]

This tendency of the educationists to enhance their position and consolidate their power is one of the reasons I feel we should approach with caution the question of federal aid to education which many Americans feel is the only device that can wipe out unequal educational opportunities. In view of the simple truth, which has been stated by the Supreme Court, that the state is bound "to regulate that which it subsidizes," we may well ask ourselves who the regulators will be; the answer, unfortunately, is that they will be the educationists. Federal aid will be the final step which will put the

---

17. In this paragraph I have drawn on an excellent article which I recommend to my readers, "Educational Administration and Responsible Government," by Ernest A. Engelbert, *School and Society*, January 19, 1952.

educationists in undisputed control of American public school education. To some it seems like a very high price to pay for equalization of opportunities.

Even if we get equalization of opportunity I do not think we can be assured that it will mean actual improvement in *quality* of education, if the educationists are to set the tone. In the field of Negro education, for example, the southern states have (largely under threat of what has now come to pass, nonsegregation) made tremendous strides in recent years in improving facilities but it remains to be seen if these mechanical advances mean a comparable advance in standards when the standards are set by the educationists. A recent article in a professional magazine, characteristically titled "A High School Diploma for All!" may show which way the wind is blowing. In this article, which describes an "experiment" carried on in a Negro high school in Alabama with the approval of the state department of education, the author rehashes the old familiar arguments about the curriculum being based on the "needs" of the students; as the majority of students in this school become farmers, farmers' wives, or domestics, they don't need to master "theoretical" material, such as history, mathematics, and science but need to learn "socially acceptable manners" and " a few facts, skills, and habits and the acceptance of a few ruling principles." The experiment consists in "awarding a high school diploma to any student who has spent three years in high school. . . . Scholastic achievement is no longer the basis for awarding the diploma."[18] In other words, it's the old trick of the educationists of dividing the sheep and the goats; an attempt will be made to educate the minority who plan to go to college—the sheep—but as for

18. J. D. Thompson, "A High School Diploma for All!" *The School Executive,* February, 1954.

the majority—the goats—they will have to be content with being adjusted to the lowly status they apparently are destined to occupy.

Believers in educational standards who feel that equalization of opportunities can only be achieved by federal aid and who are not, as I confess I am, frightened by state regulation *per se,* ought to give more thought than they seem to be giving to the circumstance that those who will do the regulating under federal aid are those who consistently fight to adulterate standards. One might be less concerned if there was any prospect that the regulators would include those who believe in real education, the scholars in the humanities and the sciences; this prospect is not even dim, but nonexistent. I presume that the U.S. Office of Education would fall heir to the bureaucratic functions of federal aid, but if we are really concerned with the improvement of quality wouldn't it be shortsighted to enhance the power of an office which sponsors Life Adjustment, a program based on the assumption that the majority of Americans are incapable of absorbing education?

My severe criticism here of professional education will, as it has on other occasions, undoubtedly be deplored as discourteous in tone and lacking in the spirit of cooperation and conciliation; perhaps some readers will excuse it as a necessary part of the hygiene of the traditionalist, as an aid to circulation of his blood, which is the way Logan Pearsall Smith described the denunciation of the young by the old. Be that as it may, I have felt under the necessity of speaking unequivocally about a situation which is adversely affecting the health of the American public school system and is, unfortunately, but dimly comprehended by the great majority of parents and laymen. When laymen will take the trouble to inform themselves I think they will come to understand the monolithic nature of professional education and will agree with Paul Wood-ring (one of those rare individuals, a professor in a school of education who is skeptical of current fashions) when he says that under the present system the individual who holds to a minority point of view "is treated as a backward child who must be brought to see the light," that "permanent nonagreement is never tolerated," and that "the validity of pragmatic principles" is never questioned.[19]

How this stranglehold of the professionals on public education works in concrete instances, particularly how it works in dealing with parental and lay criticism of the schools, will be the subject of the next chapter.

---

19. *Let's Talk Sense About Our Schools* (New York; McGraw-Hill, 1953).

VI

Putting Parents in Their Place, or, The Customer Is Always Wrong

In the face of widespread criticism of the American public school what is the attitude of the professional educators who are responsible for the character of the system? If only a small portion of that criticism is valid one would think they might well be chastened, that they might make some efforts at internal reform. Unfortunately, the mood of most educators, far from being contrite, seems to be composed partly of uncritical satisfaction with what they are doing and partly of bellicosity towards anyone who doubts the current dogmas. The tendency to question the motives of all critics of schools is probably for the most part sincere, for the complacency of educators is such that they are frankly incredulous when faced with the fact that some persons question their system.

Any scholar or teacher outside the ranks of professional education who ventures criticism is immediately belittled and denounced—and on occasion attempts are even made to suppress him. Take, for example, the case of Arthur E. Bestor, Jr., professor of history at the University of Illinois, whose book *Educational Wastelands* is a brilliant and well documented description of what he calls the retreat from learning in our public schools. It is possible, of course, to disagree with Professor Bestor's diagnosis but he is a serious, scholarly, and responsible critic who has the support of hundreds of other reputable scholars in all subject fields in his avowed aim of exposing the weaknesses of the schools and proposing remedies.[1]

It was perhaps inevitable that Professor Bestor should be called names by the educationists, and he was, among them faultfinder, complainer, exceedingly naive, publicity seeker, and superficial. It was perhaps also inevitable that he should be answered by two professors of education sponsored by four professional educational committees who managed to use thirty-seven pages of small type in rebuttal without ever coming to grips with his main argument.[2] The situation being what it is, these were conventional reactions; what is surprising, and not a little disturbing, is the fact that educators have made strenuous efforts to shut off Bestor's means of public

---

1. In December, 1952, Professor Bestor presented to the American Historical Association a strongly-worded resolution condemning anti-intellectualism in the schools and calling upon the Association to join with other learned societies to form a Permanent Scientific and Scholarly Commission whose function would be to undertake an over-all study of the schools and to make recommendations for reforms. This resolution, which was tabled for study, was supported by over six hundred scholars including such well-known figures as Arthur M. Schlesinger, Sr., Samuel F. Bemis, Carlton J. H. Hayes, James G. Randall, C. Vann Woodward, Charles W. Cole, Merle Curti, Samuel Eliot Morison, and Allan Nevins.

2. See "A Scholar's Documents" by Harold C. Hand and Charles W. Sanford, the *Bulletin* of the National Association of Secondary-School Principals, April, 1953, pp. 460–504. This was prepared "in collaboration" with the Executive Committee of the National Association of Secondary-School Principals, the Curriculum Planning and Development Committee of the same association, the Executive Committee of the Illinois Curriculum Program, and the National Commission on Life Adjustment Education for Youth.

expression. In the September 19, 1953, issue of *School and Society* (perhaps the best, certainly the least doctrinaire of educational journals) there appeared an article of his called "On the Education and Certification of Teachers" in which he made several proposals for the reform of teacher training, his main contention being that a new curriculum for teacher education, based on the liberal arts and sciences "rather than upon the mere vocational skills of pedagogy" is necessary to restore the repute of the public schools. Possibly this contention, and some of his proposals in support of it, might be debatable; but the educators didn't want to debate with Bestor, they wanted to suppress him. One of the most influential educationists in the country, dean of a school of education, circularized the members of the National Society of College Teachers of Education urging that they make "a vigorous protest" to the editor and trustees of *School and Society* against "opening the columns" of that magazine to what he called Bestor's "scurrilous, demagogic and dishonest" article. His comment that "Bestor and that aggregation of academic politicians are just as ambitious to take over for their own purposes the education of teachers as is Senator McCarthy to take over and rule, either officially or unofficially" is, of course, an irresponsible and foolish statement but rather amusing coming, as it does, from a leading representative of the great entrenched monopoly in American education. According to the editor, almost all those who followed the dean's suggestion and wrote in to protest "voiced a vehement denial of Bestor's right to be heard in *School and Society*."[3]

---

3. For a history of this controversy see the following issues of *School and Society*: September 19, November 14, November 29, 1953, and January 23, 1954. In a later issue of this magazine (February 6, 1954) Dean Francis Keppel of the Graduate School of

Another attempt at suppression—and this time a successful one—involved Frank Richardson, until June, 1953, chairman of the biology department at the University of Nevada and head of the local chapter of the American Association of University Professors. When the university's new president, a former professor of education, announced that he thought emphasis on the academic subjects was "intellectual snobbery" and that in the future all graduates of Nevada high schools, regardless of academic standing, would be admitted to the university, Professor Richardson entered a strong protest against such adulteration of standards. He was then promptly accused by the president of being "insubordinate" and "a buttinsky all over the campus" and at the request of the president was dismissed from his post by the Board of Regents. Such is the arrogance of the dedicated educationist.[4]

In the opinion of the majority of educators there just isn't

Education, Harvard University, defended Bestor's right to be heard and denied that he could be fairly accused of being unfriendly "toward the basic political purpose of public education and the right of the children of each generation to educational opportunity." However, the dean felt Bestor was not without responsibility for "creating a querulous atmosphere" and also thought he was "far from courteous" in his comments about professors of education. For the rest, he thinks Bestor's idea of education is too narrowly intellectual, and seems to feel that Bestor wouldn't agree that "learning decent behavior, honesty, how to live by democratic values, etc.," is a task of the school as well as the home. I am sure that Professor Bestor, along with other critics of modern education, would agree that these things have always, and rightfully, been a part of the school's task, but perhaps were better performed before they became "subjects" and were simply a natural concomitance of learning and classroom atmosphere.

4. See *Time*, June 15, 1953, p. 50; *Newsweek*, June 22, 1953, p. 86; and various articles in the *San Francisco Chronicle* in May, June, and July, 1953.

any academic critic of the schools whose argument is objective or whose motive is honest. As I. L. Kandel, himself a professor of education but an unorthodox one, has said, "The critic, however sincere, who ventures to comment adversely on the consequences of the cult of pragmatism, experimentalism, or instrumentalism is regarded as almost committing sacrilege."[5] This is borne out by the educationist who disposes of a whole bevy of such academic critics by asking if "the frenetic fulminations of the Maritains, the Barzuns, the Bells, the DeVotos, the Van Dorens and their kind" are to be explained "merely as a hangover of the aristocratic tradition or the smug complacency of the narrowminded?"[6]

If the educators resent the criticisms of their colleagues in the humanities departments the ultimate profanation in their eyes seems to be lay criticism. Occasionally they are lenient with it but they never acknowledge its validity; one dean of a college of education announced that he had investigated the past record of the author of this book and one other lay writer on education and found that we belonged to no "subversive" or "self-centered" groups, and that while we are, of course, prejudiced and unscholarly, "I cannot say that they are unscrupulous."[7] (Do I only imagine that the professor's tone is dripping with regret?) Professor Robert R. Sears, recently of

5. *School and Society,* August 22, 1953.

6. William Clark Trow, "The Public School a Scapegoat?" School of Education *Bulletin,* The University of Michigan, November, 1951. I am aware of the fact that Bernard DeVoto is capable on occasion of being a frenetic fulminator but do not know when he has turned his wrath on the public schools. He is the author of a delicious spoofing of progressive education, "Parable of the Lost Chance," *Harper's Magazine,* January, 1950.

7. Willard B. Spalding, "The Stereotype of Progressive Education in the Profession and in the Public," *Progressive Education,* November, 1951.

the Harvard Graduate School of Education is more harsh; he has said that laymen who criticize the schools are "among the emotionally least stable members of the community. They are likely to be the ones who have had family difficulties of their own, who have had trouble rearing their own children, who have exhibited their bigotry and excitability in connection with other community activities. . . ."[8] On the other hand, another member of the same school of education, William H. Burton, feels that criticisms by parents "are practically always honest and sincere but"—here's the rub—"nearly always have no factual basis."[9] It's a hard choice for the lay critic but there seems no alternative—either you're an emotionally unbalanced bigot or a sincere ignoramus.

With such an attitude towards lay criticism almost universal among the educators, it is perhaps inevitable that the various parents' groups which have sprung up across the country during the post-war years should come in for some rough handling from the professionals. The members of these groups have been accused of being tax-resisters, reactionaries, enemies of public education, and part of a national conspiracy against public schools headed by Allen A. Zoll. (Zoll is a professional agitator of the Gerald L.K. Smith type whose present venture is something called the National Council for American Education.) As the educators have all the big publicity guns—principally the literature, magazines, conventions, and commissions associated with the National Education Association and its numerous subsidiary organizations—it has been extremely easy for the educator-bloc to present

---

8. *Official Report,* The American Association of School Administrators, 1952.

9. "Get the Facts: Both Ours and the Other Fellow's!" *Progressive Education,* January, 1952.

whatever picture they want to present to the American public of the nature of these parents groups. What they have chosen to do, through an official and widespread campaign, is to pillory and discredit sincere people who believe in public education but cannot follow the party line.

Having met or corresponded with many of these parents groups across the country, I can testify that being human they are not comprised exclusively of people of superlative wisdom and tact; but I think it is accurate to say that most of the people in these groups are responsible, decent citizens, free of fanatical and lunatic urges, who are united in feeling that the public schools have gone wrong somewhere and ought to be set right. I did not meet anyone among them who was opposed to school spending *per se,* or anyone who wanted to return in school matters to the supposedly better days of 1900. None of the groups of which I have personal knowledge used any literature issued by Zoll's organization except the group in Pasadena in the early months of its existence and they quickly withdrew the material when they discovered the facts about his record. (In one town—Eugene, Oregon—they were so frightened of being tainted by Zoll that they made a ceremony of burning the pamphlets he had, unsolicited, sent to them.) The members of these groups range, ideologically, from liberal to extreme conservative; in one college town the group of protesting parents was almost exclusively egg-head intellectuals of New Dealish persuasion while in another town one earnest lady in the group took me aside to inquire if I had detected any evidence of subversive tendencies in the Scottish Rites of the Masons. (I haven't.) In other words, the gamut is pretty broad, so broad that it is patently absurd to try, as the educators have, to pin the same tag on all of the members of these groups.

As an illustration of how these groups are treated at the hands of the professionals it might be illuminating to recount the experiences of the Citizens Schools Committee of Los Angeles. What happened in this case is fairly typical of the experiences of parents groups in other towns and cities.

Under the superintendency of Alexander J. Stoddard the schools of Los Angeles have been consistently "modern," understandably so, for Mr. Stoddard was for ten years chairman of the Educational Policies Commission of the NEA whose publication *Education for All American Youth* (1944) is part of the official scriptures of those schoolmen who believe that the primary task of the schools is no longer the inculcation of knowledge but social adjustment.[10] A small group of Los Angeles residents who suspected that all was not well with the local schools began meeting in the late fall of 1949 as a study group, their object being to learn something about the theory and practice of the local system. None of them seemed to be emotionally unstable, excitable, or bigoted and there wasn't a super-patriot or tax-resister in the lot; on the contrary one would have said they comprised an unusually pleasant, well-adjusted, and intelligent group. One woman was the wife of a well-known doctor; one was a lecturer on music and the symphony concerts; another was a trustee of Leland Stanford; another was a university professor. Of the men, one was head of a film construction union, one president of a baking company, another assistant trade commissioner of the Nether-

10. Mr. Stoddard came to Los Angeles from the superintendency of schools in Philadelphia. His last two years in that city were marked by controversy about progressive policies in the schools, culminating in a public protest from the combined faculties of fourteen of the city's sixteen high schools against the policy of automatic promotion, described by the teachers as a "something-for-nothing" policy. See *Time*, August 18, 1947.

lands, and another held an important university post. None of them was out to prove that the schools are communistic and none of them knew Allen Zoll from a hole in the wall. They were even able to pronounce the words progressive education without hissing; one member of the group, pointing out that they were not opposed to all phases of progressive education, said: "The new attention to individual differences in capacity and in rates of growth in children cannot be praised too highly; and to bring life and interest into what may have been learning by rote is a most desirable achievement."[11]

The group spent several months in study of the schools; they observed classroom procedures, had conferences with principals, supervisors, assistant superintendents and with Mr. Stoddard, and they read widely in educational literature, especially the various publications of the NEA and its subsidiaries. The result of their work was a firm conviction that the Los Angeles schools, especially on the elementary level, were practicing a form of progressive, or modern, education which overemphasized adjustment and neglected learning. Their

---

11. It is important to point out that the Citizens Schools Committee had nothing whatsoever to do with the agitation in 1951 and 1952 which caused the Los Angeles Board of Education to withdraw a teaching manual about UNESCO and to withdraw also from a United Nations essay contest. This seems to have been accomplished in large part through the efforts of an energetic lady named Florence Fowler Lyons who had no connection of any kind with the Citizens Schools Committee. The Committee also played no part in the refusal in 1953 of the Board of Education to accept a grant from the Ford Foundation for a teacher-training experiment, except that their member on the Board, Arthur Gardner, was the only one to vote for its acceptance. (Some members of the Board felt they had discovered socialistic tendencies in the Ford Foundation.)

feeling about the situation was perhaps adequately summed up by one member of the group who said, "We used to take Mary to the zoo, and the school taught her arithmetic. Now we teach her arithmetic, and the school takes her to the zoo."

Only after six months of study, and after conferences which convinced them that the school administration intended to do nothing about it, did the Citizens Schools Committee decide to air the issue publicly. In May, 1950, they issued a statement which charged that the Los Angeles schools were neglecting fundamental subject matter in favor of a program of social adjustment which they felt to be of doubtful value; they felt, specifically, that grammar, arithmetic, history, geography, and penmanship were being neglected and they considered that the sight-reading method had proved unsuccessful in teaching children to read. Their opinion seemed to be confirmed by the results of school tests; some light was thrown on the ability of Los Angeles students in the fundamentals by the results of Iowa Tests in achievement administered to the 10th grade in the years 1948, 1949, and 1950. While they ranked high nationally in capacity, their composite scores in achievement for those years was 43, 40, and 44. These scores being in percentile form, this means that in 1950 they were exceeded in achievement by 56 per cent of students tested nationally. At the same time, only 20 per cent exceeded them in capacity for learning. In one subject, arithmetic, their score in 1950 was 8—that is, they were exceeded by 92 per cent of all students tested. (For other information on the state of education in Los Angeles see page 16.)

The committee soon discovered, by the avalanche of letters which descended on them in answer to their publicity, that thousands of Los Angeles citizens were dissatisfied with the school system. The same complaints appeared over and over again: children couldn't read or spell or figure and they were undisciplined. In answer, the president of the Board of Education said that the committee was "attacking teachers and children" and the superintendent said he hoped the people of Los Angeles would have the good sense not to take such an attack seriously.[12] He also suggested that the schools in the United States were under attack by persons who believe in the "master race concept," who don't want a program fitted to individual needs, who think education should be for the select few, and who want to turn the school system backward to the days of 1900 or even 1850.[13] He was quick to add that of course he wasn't referring to the Citizens Schools Committee. During the next few months this sort of oblique attack became more open and the committee, which supposed it was working for the improvement of public education, found itself accused of being part of a sinister nation-wide attack on the schools. At the NEA convention at St. Louis in July, Harold Benjamin, chairman of the National Commission for the Defense of Democracy Through Education, said that "the enemy" had "started an all-out campaign which he is supporting with every weapon in his arsenal" in the Los Angeles-Pasadena-Glendale area. According to Mr. Benjamin the Los

12. Apparently some three years later the superintendent and the board decided that charges of deficiencies in the three R's *were* to be taken seriously. According to the *Los Angeles Times* of October 2, 1953, Superintendent Stoddard reported that as tests over a period of three years showed definite deficiencies he recommended, and the board accepted, a plan to set up "teams" of principals and teachers—at a cost of almost $100,000—who will study the situation "and tell us what we can do about teaching our children better." It didn't seem to occur to the superintendent that a lot of time-tested, if neglected, information in that field is already available.

13. *Los Angeles Times,* May 19, 1950.

Angeles committee and similar committees were going into full-scale battle "under the steam of that indignation about spending money for a modern school program, garnished with a variety of pretty, little cultivated indignations about William H. Kilpatrick's sinister influence and the spread of atheism nurtured by fads and frills." As far as the Los Angeles committee was concerned, this was a complete misrepresentation for the committee had never made any protests about the spending of money or any charges of atheism, and although it wouldn't have been necessary for them to cultivate indignation about Kilpatrick's influence as they were already feeling pretty disturbed about it, it so happened that his name had never been mentioned in any of their publicity.

The Parent-Teacher Associations, which usually bend double trying to avoid "controversial" issues, faced up to this one bravely: they were violent in their denunciations of the committee. This was perhaps not surprising for PTA's everywhere are apt to be dominated by the school administration; and in this case the president of the combined PTA's of the city happened to be the wife of the president of the Board of Education. When *McCall's* published an article titled "Who's Trying to Ruin Our Schools?" in which it was declared that Allen Zoll was a "potent influence in every city where schools have come under attack" and stated specifically that Zoll's "philosophy" was being advocated by the Citizens Schools Committee of Los Angeles, the article was recommended by every local PTA in the city.[14] It was also recommended in the bulletin of the Affiliated Teachers of Los Angeles which is the local branch of the NEA, and the latter organization also kindly supplied the CIO weekly magazine, *Light,* with a list of organ-

14. Arthur D. Morse, "Who's Trying to Ruin Our Schools?" *McCall's,* September, 1951.

izations which were "attacking" the schools, including of course the name of the Los Angeles committee.

Before making such charges the NEA never made any effort to talk with any members of the committee nor apparently made any open investigation of it. However, the secretary of the committee has often wondered since what was the purpose of a young man who called on her one day who said he was collecting material for his doctoral thesis which was to be on the subject of citizens' committees. Asking permission to use a tape recorder because he wrote slowly, he then asked such questions as: "Do you have any connection with other committees in other cities? What do you think about school taxes? What do you think of racial minorities?" The secretary replied amiably that her committee had no affiliation with other committees but had corresponded with some of them, that she thought schools should have plenty of money, and that she was very fond of her Japanese neighbors. (The young man did not inform her at the time that he was a "curriculum co-ordinator" in the school system of a neighboring city.)

It is reasonable to suppose that the professionals did their best to find something damaging about the committee but the only definite thing they could charge them with was a somewhat less than heinous crime; they "admitted having corresponded with other committees."[15] But as a result of these efforts to prove that the parents group was motivated by dis-

---

15. The author of this book must plead guilty to being an accessory before the fact in the commission of this offence. After a member of the Citizens Schools Committee had been good enough to write me about my book, *And Madly Teach*, I sent her the names of several other parents groups who had also written to me about their dissatisfaction with the schools. The fact that these groups then exchanged stories of their experiences apparently constitutes conspiracy in the eyes of the educators.

honorable aims the real issue, whether the Los Angeles schools are doing a good or a poor job, was obscured, and a totally synthetic issue raised. A group of public spirited citizens who took seriously the educators' admonition to Know Your Schools was brought up sharply to the realization that the invitation doesn't include the right to advocate any changes.

A similar pattern to the one in Los Angeles followed the formation of parents groups in other sections of the country. Early in 1950 a Parents' Council was formed in Minneapolis having as its chief objective the elimination of the Common Learnings program, or at least making it optional. This was something which had been inaugurated in the Minneapolis schools when Willard Goslin had been superintendent and was the usual attempt to substitute for formal subject matter an activity program which would give students "the skills of living and working together effectively." In Denver, where a similar program called General Education had been introduced by Superintendent Kenneth Oberholtzer, it was opposed by the Denver Citizens' Committee for Public Schools. In Eugene, Oregon, a Parents' Council for Education was formed and in Montgomery County, Maryland, a Parents' League for Curriculum Improvement. Roughly the aims of all these groups were the same; they all wanted more emphasis on reading, spelling, grammar, handwriting, arithmetic, history, and geography; they wanted better classroom discipline, the restoration of report cards with grades, and standard tests for promotion. It is, of course, possible to argue that these are not adequate aims for education, or bad aims, and if you think so then Benjamin Fine's criticism of the Los Angeles committee, that its demands would turn the educational clock back a good half century, may seem a devastating one.[16] But

16. *The New York Times,* January 18, 1952. Mr. Fine is education editor of the *Times.*

the educators were not content with making this criticism, and trying to substantiate it; to them the parents were not only wrong, they were villainous. There followed on the formation of each committee a concerted effort to belittle it and impugn its motives.

As a demonstration of just how powerful the professional machinery can be when it gets rolling, the classic example, of course, is the now famous Pasadena case involving the forced resignation in 1950 of Willard E. Goslin as superintendent of schools. The battle of the schools in that West Coast city is an old story now but unfortunately a distorted one; probably most Americans who do not attempt to keep themselves informed about public education have the vague impression that the Pasadena affair involved the martyrdom of an able, idealistic educator at the hands of a sinister, reactionary and fascistic national organization. There is a good deal of evidence that this is exactly the impression many professional educators hope the majority of Americans have of the Pasadena affair; certainly they tried hard at the time to create this impression. An investigation made by the author of this book in Pasadena convinces him that skillful professional propaganda created a legend, the legend of the good administrator and the bad committee, which, like all legends, does not bear up well when the harsh light of historical fact is thrown on it.

The story of Pasadena begins roughly in late 1947 when the board of education of that city began the search for a new superintendent of schools to replace John A. Sexson who was retiring after twenty years of service. Unfortunately, like too many boards of education, this one seems to have been more interested in securing a "dynamic" public figure than in trying to arrive among themselves at some consistent philosophy of education and then searching for a man to carry it out. Willard

E. Goslin, the man they chose (then superintendent in Minneapolis) was and is the archetype of the dynamic public figure. Always active in NEA politics, he was at the time of coming to Pasadena, president of the auxiliary organization, the American Association of School Administrators. He is an impressive speaker in a somewhat oratorical, evangelistic manner; utilizing a Missouri drawl and a deliberately non-highbrow presentation replete with homely expressions, he can move a convention to frenzied enthusiasm. Educationally, he is a wholehearted modernist who uses all the shibboleths of the cult although his devotion seems perhaps more sentimental than philosophical. In short, Mr. Goslin is a typical figure thrown up by the politics of the managerial group in American public education: ambitious, anti-intellectual, one might almost say, anti-educational.

Obviously the Pasadena board of education didn't see Mr. Goslin in this light; they liked his "personality" and they hired him. Mr. Goslin was happy to accept and probably glad to leave Minneapolis where there were increasing parental rumblings against his educational program. (There had also been, through no fault of his, a strike of the entire teaching body during his administration.) Two years after his hiring, the board requested Goslin's resignation on the grounds that as "the main controversy in Pasadena settles around you as an individual," peace could only be restored if he stepped out. Although it is true that some of the dissatisfaction with the superintendent arose from what many considered defects of temperament and administrative ineptness, the board of education seems never to have grasped the fact that primarily the majority of the people of their city didn't like the extremist position Mr. Goslin took in education. Although the board knew there had been much uneasiness under the sort of progressive education which had been introduced in Pasadena by Dr. Sexson, they decided to hire as his successor a man who, as a member of the Progressive Education Association and the John Dewey Society, could hardly be expected to reverse the educational trend. A good deal of the blame for the Pasadena fiasco rests with the board of education for failure to evaluate the educational views of the community and to seek a man who might, at least approximately, share those views.[17]

Not long after Goslin came to Pasadena a group of citizens who were unhappy about school matters formed the School Development Council. Although their dissatisfaction was partly a hangover from the regime of Dr. Sexson, they soon found much to disapprove of in the new administration. Automatic promotions, abolition of graded report cards, the elimination of systematic learning in core programs, the discussion of complex national and international affairs among children who seemed to have little grounding in fundamental knowledge and information—which were features of both the old

---

17. This is perhaps easier said than done, in view of the system which everywhere prevails in the selection of superintendents. The president of the Pasadena board said that they had applied to various colleges of education for suggestions in selecting their new superintendent and that in the case of all the candidates they interviewed "their philosophy was very much the same." (See Eighth Report, California State Investigating Committee on Education, "Education in Pasadena," p. 17.) As boards of education must depend on the dossiers prepared by the placement bureaus of the colleges of education, and as the colleges of education won't recommend a man who doesn't follow the official line, the traditionalist in education has small chance of landing a superintendency. Some, of course, have been known to pay only lip service to the revealed faith and after getting in office have surreptitiously introduced some traditional concepts of education.

and new regimes—came in for much criticism, but there were special complaints against Goslin. One of the bitterest ones involved William H. Kilpatrick who was brought to Pasadena by Goslin to spend four days talking to a "workshop" of teachers and administrators. That prophet of distorted Deweyism came and displayed his usual ragbag of vague educational clichés; there was the inaccurate caricature of traditional education, the airy painting of the delights of the child-centered school, the belittling of formal knowledge, the usual smattering of questionable sociological, historical, and economic tidbits, the usual suggestion that a lot of horrid "ins" are exploiting a lot of nice "outs." Perhaps most people in the School Development Council were willing to let Dr. Kilpatrick have his say but they were concerned by the assumption on the part of the administration that what he had to say constituted a sound guide for Pasadena. In the introduction to Kilpatrick's printed remarks Superintendent Goslin wrote: "In company with other leaders, Dr. Kilpatrick has had opposition to some of his views. However, parents, teachers, and other citizens who have taken the time to study and understand his proposals have very generally supported them." Aside from the fact that they thought this statement would be difficult to substantiate, the members of the SDC felt that it sounded very much as if their superintendent favored the extreme wing of progressive educational thought and would attempt to introduce its practices in the Pasadena schools.

The SDC also didn't like the fact that Goslin had brought with him from Minneapolis as deputy superintendent in charge of curriculum a man who was a director of the American Education Fellowship (formerly the Progressive Education Association) of which one of the aims was "to channel the energy of the educators towards the reconstruction of the economic system."[18] Their feelings of agitation were not quieted when Goslin invited Theodore Brameld to speak in Pasadena for by now they had delved sufficiently into American education to know that Professor Brameld is the leading advocate among schoolmen of the theory that education should be an instrument of indoctrination in behalf of a reconstructed social and economic order. Probably most of the members of the SDC were conservatives and undoubtedly some of them could be called reactionaries in the sense that they were wary of all change, but in any case they were all united in feeling that they didn't want America "reconstructed" in the Brameld sense and certainly didn't want the schools used for this purpose. For that matter probably the overwhelming majority of the people of Pasadena, if they stopped to think about it, would have been against the American Education Fellowship's and Professor Brameld's view that education should seek to transform the economic and social order.

During the first year and a half, then, of Goslin's incumbency dissatisfactions were building up on two scores: a great many people felt that he favored an even more extreme form of progressive education than had prevailed under his predecessor, and they felt that he tended to be sympathetic to the social reconstructionist school. There is some evidence to

---

18. In September, 1953, the American Education Fellowship assumed its old name of the Progressive Education Association. Somewhere along the line it seems to have lost its aim of reconstructing the economic system. This aim used to be stated on the back cover of its magazine *Progressive Education* but has now been abandoned in favor of one which states that members are "committed to the democratic ideal and devoted to the continuous reconstruction of education for the fuller realization of that ideal in school and society."

show that members of the SDC were willing to argue out these issues with the superintendent and the board of education, but in the spring of 1950 something happened that made them decide to declare public war: Mr. Goslin and the board asked for an election to raise the school tax. Under California law the schools are partly supported by state aid and partly by taxes levied by local school districts on assessed value of real estate; in Pasadena the legal maximum that could be levied was $0.90 for each $100 of assessed valuation. Mr. Goslin figured that to meet the requirements of his budget for the coming school year he would need an increase of $0.30 per $100 but he convinced the school board that they should ask for $0.45, or in other words, an increase in the school tax of 50 per cent. It was explained that while this amount was not needed immediately it would be needed in the future, and to have it all voted at once would eliminate the bother of later elections.

The SDC decided to fight the tax rise on the basis that they didn't want to pay additional taxes for something with which they were already dissatisfied. The members realized, as their chairman said, that "a repudiation of the proposed school tax would be at the same time a repudiation of Goslin and his program." There followed several weeks of the bitterest sort of public controversy with the result that twice as many people as had ever voted before in a school election turned out to defeat Goslin's proposed tax by the impressive vote of 22,212 to 10,032. That this was pretty much an anti-Goslin vote and not resistance to taxes *per se* is shown by the fact that the year after Goslin left Pasadena a school tax increase from $0.90 to $1.22 was passed without serious opposition.

During the debate one member of the SDC discovered a pamphlet called "Progressive Education *Increases* Delinquency" by Allen A. Zoll. Although its tone was deliberately sensational and in it Mr. Zoll made some rather absurd statements about educational pragmatists and seemed to be laboring under the delusion that Robert Hutchins is a believer in progressive education, the pamphlet as a whole had some perfectly valid generalizations to make about the influence of pragmatism on education, so the SDC ordered a batch from the willing salesman and distributed them at one public meeting. Almost immediately they learned that Mr. Zoll had been an associate of such unlovely characters as Father Coughlin and Gerald L.K. Smith and that one of his earlier organizations had been on the Attorney General's list as "fascist and subversive." Although the SDC had never before heard of Zoll and withdrew the pamphlet as soon as they realized they had been duped, they had already committed the fatal act, the tactical blunder, which was to set in motion the legend that has been carefully nurtured by the educators ever since, the legend that the SDC was a pawn in the hands of a sinister national conspiracy aimed at the destruction of the American public school.

The introduction of the Zoll issue added to the noise and confusion of a campaign already full of charges and counter charges but essentially the issue in the Pasadena affair was not complex. It can finally be reduced to this: so many people became dissatisfied with Willard Goslin that his position as superintendent simply became untenable. The reasons for dissatisfaction were not all based on his educational philosophy, either. When the board of education finally requested his resignation, some months after the tax election, they seemed more irritated by what they considered high-handed administrative tactics than by matters relating solely to education. There were widespread complaints by parents, principals, and teachers that he rarely visited the schools and made little effort to know school personnel. Even the investigating committee sent to Pasadena by the NEA sometime after Goslin's resignation—a committee presumably anxious to give Goslin every benefit of the doubt—felt that he alienated the local press, unnecessarily ignored influential people in the community, held himself aloof from the general public, and used poor judgment in launching his tax program.[19] The general feeling around Pasadena, a feeling by no means entirely confined to his enemies, was that Willard Goslin's mind was on higher things, that his overpowering ambition was to be a national figure in education. When all these feelings of dissatisfaction became intense enough Goslin's exit from the picture became inevitable. But the dissatisfactions were not synthetic, imported ones—they were homegrown and very real.

It would be foolish to maintain that all virtue resided in the SDC which played such an important part in this battle. Some of its members were undoubtedly ultra-conservatives who were ready enough to confuse liberalism with communism and some of them seemed to think that patriotism was something they invented and on which they held the patent. (They were confirmed in their dark suspicions of communist influence when the *People's World* and various communist fronts praised Goslin and denounced the SDC although the pro-Goslinites certainly didn't want, and were acutely embarrassed by, communist support.) One Pasadena teacher who is herself antiprogressive said to me that too many members of the SDC objected to modern education on no higher grounds than that

19. *The Pasadena Story*, An Analysis of Some Forces and Factors That Injured a Superior School System, National Commission for the Defense of Democracy Through Education of the National Education Association, June, 1951, pp. 24–26, 33–35.

"some books mentioned a country called Russia and some of the movies used in the classrooms implied that storks did not bring babies." But despite the occasional foolishness of some of its individual members and some errors of strategy and emphasis (due primarily to the circumstance that this was an improvised, amateur committee, not versed in the arts of public relations), the SDC was comprised of good people, honest and sincere citizens whose concern about the nature and the quality of public education in their city quite naturally involved them in a controversy with the responsible head of the schools.

The national hierarchy of educationists refused to accept the simple truth that a sufficient number of people got angry enough at modern education to cause the ouster of one of its high priests. Again, the assumption seemed to be that any group who would do *that* must naturally be evil. There then began the intense campaign to launch the legend of the brave good knight of modern education attacked by the forces of darkness. Even before Goslin resigned, Harold Benjamin, at the same NEA meeting where he had put the Los Angeles committee in its place, had this to say: "In the recent Pasadena case, anti-tax groups, heated 'patriots,' and opponents of Columbia University's 'red' pragmatism rallied behind a general, or chief-of-staff, named Allen A. Zoll." It was at this meeting that Mr. Benjamin coined the phrase "the enemy" which has since become the general epithet applied by many educators to those who don't accept the revealed gospel.[20]

Sometime later a pamphlet with the scary title *Danger!*

---

20. Mr. Benjamin's pronouncement received enormous publicity throughout the country and was later widely circulated as Defense Bulletin No. 35 of the National Commission for the Defense of Democracy Through Education.

They're After Our Schools was issued by this imposing list of sponsors: American Association of Colleges for Teacher Education, Committee on Tenure and Academic Freedom, Department of Classroom Teachers, Department of Higher Education, National Association of Secondary-School Principals, Commission for the Defense of Democracy Through Education—all affiliated with the NEA—and the American Jewish Committee and the John Dewey Society. One would think that such an important and influential group would be very careful with matters of fact even if idealogically they were opposed to such committees as the Pasadena SDC but in at least two respects this pamphlet grossly misrepresents the Pasadena situation. The false, and by now regulation, charge is made that Zoll's literature "played an important part in bringing about the resignation of Dr. Willard Goslin," although this statement is in flat contradiction of the views held by Robert A. Skaife, secretary of one of the sponsoring organizations, the National Commission for the Defense of Democracy Through Education. Mr. Skaife, who made a personal investigation for his commission right after the tax election, wrote to Willard Goslin on June 26, 1950, as follows: "Visits to newspaper and realty men convince me that the Zoll materials were but a small factor in the 22,000 'No' votes cast in the election." He also stated in the same letter that there were strong indications "that those who voted 'No' did not vote 'No' because of Zoll materials. School people have not faced this."[21]

Danger! They're After Our Schools also states that "the in-

---

21. See *Los Angeles Times*, March 3, 1952, "New Light Brought to Goslin Ousting," by Chester G. Hanson. Also see "What Really Happened in Pasadena?" by Oliver Carlson, the *Freeman*, July 30, 1951.

habitants [of Pasadena] will suffer for years to come from an onslaught which robbed their community of an outstanding educator." One of the ways the community will suffer, suggests the pamphlet, is that now no one will have the courage to speak up and say that "an expansion program is needed" for the schools. "Few teachers would risk Dr. Goslin's fate by suggesting that Pasadena's first-rate youngsters are not getting first-rate schooling. . . . Education per child costs less— and each child gets less education." Passing over the typical educationist notion that more money automatically means better schooling, this statement would be completely invalidated had the authors of the pamphlet included a fact which they choose to ignore, namely, that sometime after Goslin's departure the citizens of Pasadena voted the school tax they rejected while he was still in office.

It is difficult to escape the conclusion that the authors of *Danger! They're After Our Schools,* despite its impressive sponsorship, permitted their impatience with criticism of the schools to weaken their grasp on facts.

Several lay writers, some of them in cooperation with the professionals, joined the latter in putting Goslin's opponents into neat, if horrid, categories. One article, by a not too strange coincidence titled "The Enemy in Pasadena," might have been thought to be of doubtful value to the cause in view of the fact that its author, Carey McWilliams, was at the time just about the West Coast's most prolific joiner of procommunist fronts. (Mr. McWilliams has since become an editor of that model of objectivity, *The Nation.*) Unfortunately, the article appeared in a reputable magazine, *The Christian Century,* and through reprints reached a wide public. An article with the loaded title "Putsch in Pasadena" by Milton A. Senn was reprinted as a pamphlet by the Anti-Defamation League of

B'nai B'rith although Mr. Senn did not make clear who was defaming who. Arthur D. Morse's now famous *McCall's* article, "Who's Trying to Ruin Our Schools?" took the official line that those opposed to Goslin were dupes of Zoll's, a point of view which surprised no one in view of the fact that much of the research for this article was done in the offices of the NEA.

The most important lay contribution to the Pasadena myth, however, was the book *This Happened in Pasadena* by David Hulburd, a reporter of excellent reputation who for twenty years was associated with the Luce publications.[22] Although the publishers of Mr. Hulburd's book state on the jacket that outside forces used Pasadena to help destroy the independence of the American public school system, and that Goslin's opposition played unwitting roles in a "calculated, far-reaching plot," the author does not attempt to sustain quite such a cloak-and-dagger atmosphere. He admits that it is a mistake to overemphasize Zoll's influence—that gentleman, of course, was happy to claim Goslin's ouster as a personal victory—but he insists that "the Zoll pattern is the same as the Pasadena pattern" by which he apparently means that because Zoll claims to be against modern education those Pasadenans who are also against certain modern educational practices must be Zoll's buddies or at least his admirers. This is not guilt by association but guilt by the holding of coincidental opinion. To indict Goslin's opponents on this basis is about as sensible as it would be to accuse all vegetarians of being anti-Semites because Hitler was also a vegetarian.

Mr. Hulburd's book is really an old-fashioned melodrama concerned with virtue and villainy. The hero is Willard Goslin and such a hero there has not been since the novels of

---

22. New York; The Macmillan Company, 1951.

Mrs. E. D. E. N. Southworth; physically, the hero is "lean and hard and fit"; his simplicity is "disarming" and he is a man of real humility and honesty, but he has "dogged determination"; he is also "a man with a mission." He is, of course, "one of the top educators in the country" and as a public speaker "he is almost without parallel." The villains, of course, are those who couldn't agree with Mr. Goslin about educational matters; they are "dissatisfied parents," "superpatriots," "ambitious, frustrated individuals"; one of them had a "nasal" voice and stumbled over words when reading in public and another is a sinister character who, when he laughs, "does so briefly and almost soundlessly." Still another is a sort of *femme fatale* who is "suave," rich in "cold hard cash," and has "many connections in the East." All of these persons belonged to that abomination of the professional, a "self-appointed" committee.[23]

Mr. Hulburd's book was received with acclaim by the professionals who did all in their not inconsiderable power to promote its circulation. It was also widely reviewed and almost universally praised by those who accepted it as literal truth. The then president of Harvard, James B. Conant (who is a good friend to public schools but sometimes overly-lenient in judging their standards) wrote a lengthy piece for the

---

23. A theory has arisen among educators in recent years that no committee is really valid unless it is appointed by some legal body. The NEA circulates widely a list prepared by Virgil Rogers, formerly a superintendent of schools and now a professor of education, which makes the attempt to distinguish honest critical groups from dishonest ones. Professor Rogers makes the statement that an honest group "has the sanction of school authorities and cooperates with local teachers and officials." As Albert Lynd has said (in *Quackery in the Public Schools*), "the irony is wholly unconscious in the insistence that a professional enterprise may not be honestly criticized without the sanction of its operators."

New York Times Book Review which was less a review than an additional salvo fired at Goslin's opponents. These Mr. Conant likened to those who "like to exert power by causing trouble, by urging the posse to lynch the victim, the mob to burn the dissenter's house, or the school board to fire the 'progressive' administrator." He, too, spoke disparagingly of "self-appointed critics of the schools" without explaining who appoints appointed critics who must, presumably, be the opposite of self-appointed ones.[24]

Thus was the Pasadena myth built up—and it is a myth which will not die. Some students of the affair feel that perhaps Mr. Hulburd and Mr. Conant, who are men of good will and integrity, may see the picture today in less stern blacks and whites; it has even been suggested that some of the top brass among the educators are no longer quite sure that all virtue was on their side. Be that as it may, the myth seems imperishable, a tribute to the power for creating propaganda by huge professional organizations—and a warning to the lowly citizen who is thinking of sticking his neck out.

There are some other lessons for parents and laymen to be derived from an understanding of what has happened in Pasadena and Los Angeles and the other communities where dissatisfied citizens have established committees. If, as happened in most of these communities, the people over a long period of time fail to interest themselves in educational philosophy and permit that philosophy to be set for them by the professionals, they are apt to suddenly wake up to the fact that they don't like what has happened during their abdication. Again, in most of these cases, the board of education had failed in their obligation to enlighten themselves about

24. "The Superintendent Was the Target," *The New York Times Book Review,* April 19, 1951.

educational theories, philosophies, and practices, to make some effort to know what the community wants in this regard, but were willing to serve largely as managers of physical plant. Where these conditions prevail, and corrective committees are formed, there is bound to be generated a certain amount of bitterness and bad feeling, for persons who are forced to fight continuously *against* something are apt to raise not only their own but their opponents' blood pressure. The tragedy is that in so many American communities parents have been forced to take up the cudgels against their own institutions.

The final lesson should now be obvious—those who set the pattern of modern public school education don't like what they call negative criticism, that is, any questioning of any of their doctrines and dogmas. If you intend to go in for any such questioning you might as well reconcile yourself to being called unpleasant names. Perhaps the better part of valor would be to take the advice of the educationist who, after telling us that determination of what is best for children is "not a matter for parents to decide, but is the responsibility of the regularly constituted school authorities" then says: "If parents do not like a public school, they can remove their children from that school and place them where conditions are more to their liking."[25] As things are going, however, it is going to be increasingly difficult to find a school which dares to be different.

Perhaps I should add a word about the accomplishment, and the fate, of the particular committees mentioned in this chapter. To mention the fate first, most of these groups are now quiescent although the Parents' Council for Education in Eugene, Oregon, continues bravely to issue a bulletin

---

25. Quoted in Fuller, "The Emperor's New Clothes," *op. cit.*

which has a good needling effect on the educators. I think it is fair to say that most of these parents' groups share a feeling of frustration and consider that their agitation has somewhat petered out, that their greatest effectiveness was shortly after they came into existence when in some cases they did exact some small concessions to their viewpoint from their local school administration. (None of the other groups were involved in anything as spectacular as the Pasadena SDC's role in the ouster of Goslin. The Los Angeles group felt it scored a minor victory when it persuaded the school board to do away with "growth reports," a substitute for the traditional graded report cards.) Most of them are pessimistic about making genuine progress, principally because they feel the educators are so strongly entrenched and the public so apathetic as to what goes on in the schools. Another discouraging factor has been that in most of these towns rival groups, encouraged and aided by the National Citizens Commission for the Public Schools, have been formed which invariably endorse the school administration and concern themselves primarily with physical plant, teachers' salaries, and public relations between school and community. This ordinarily would be all to the good but the older parents' groups feel that the newer ones, reflecting the *modus operandi* of the parent organization, lack real concern for the *quality* of education and too easily lapse into an agency for selling the schools as they are to the public. But this brings up the influence of the National Citizens Commission for the Public Schools which is another story, and one I will touch upon a little more fully in the following chapter dealing with the prospects before us.

VII

The Prospects Before Us

Over twenty years ago Albert Jay Nock ended a series of lectures on American education with the pessimistic observation that we have gone so far in the wrong direction that when we realize the need of change we will no longer have it in our power to effect the change. There are equally pessimistic prophets with us today, many of whom feel that the public schools, at least, are sunk so deep in what Robert M. Hutchins calls the four cults—skepticism, presentism, scientism, anti-intellectualism—that they must be written off as a casualty of "the spirit of the times." My own feeling is that while the picture is very dark indeed there are faint indications of brightening light along the horizon. For one thing, the frightening impasse to which we have been brought by divorcing science from spiritual wisdom—until today we stand on the brink of moral, and actually physical, disaster— is forcing some of us to a re-examination of many of the presuppositions that form the basis of the modern viewpoint, including the presuppositions of education.

One healthy sign of the times is that education is currently such a lively subject; today it is a topic of controversial discussion in a manner which was not true even ten years ago. While it does not yet rank in importance in the public mind with sex or sport, more and more people are showing some interest in the subject, are curious about theories of learning, philosophies of education, and particularly the relation of public education to the welfare of society. Books and magazine articles about education do not reach the quick oblivion that used to be their fate but are actually read and discussed. Recently New York City's municipal radio station devoted about half of its time for a week to an educational institute, and while most of the discussion was more or less open propaganda which might have been written in the offices of the NEA, the fact that it was held at all is probably a gauge of public interest. As I remarked in the Prologue to this book, there are unmistakable indications that Americans are less complacent about public education than they were before the war.

In one specific direction, the all-important matter of what sort of education should be given the future teacher, there are reasons for a cautious optimism. Recognizing that the tendency for at least thirty years has been to pay less and less attention to subject matter in the teacher's education and more and more to training in the mechanics of pedagogy, plans are now afoot for restoring a proper balance, for making the four-year liberal arts program the heart of the teacher's preparation. Various experiments in this direction are being carried on around the country with financial aid from the Ford Foundation's Fund for the Advancement of Education, notably in the State of Arkansas, where the teachers' colleges are being refashioned to approximate the program of the four-year liberal arts colleges, with training in pedagogy postponed until after graduation and integrated into the first year of teaching. More or less similar projects are being carried on at Harvard, Cornell, Wesleyan, and the University of Louisville. The reaction of the professionals to these plans has been mixed. When the Arkansas plan was first announced the American Association of Colleges for Teacher Education (a department of the NEA) called it "not only unsound but dangerous," and on the theory, apparently, that anything old is necessarily to be condemned, dubbed it "an eighteenth century model for teacher preparation." After the original bursts of antagonism there seemed to be some indications that the professionals were adopting a wait-and-see attitude, even offering a sort of passive cooperation, but as a casual reader of the professional journals I sense that in the past year the opposition has again been stiffening, as well it might, for the ultimate effect of these plans would be to deal a body-blow to the stranglehold of the educationists. Whether or not the Ford Foundation has hit on the ideal plan for teacher training may be a matter for debate but anyone who is concerned by present poor methods must be grateful that the Foundation is addressing itself to the problem at all, especially as it is not being systematically attacked elsewhere. (The educationists' own efforts at reform of their institutions are all in the direction of increasing their own influence.)

There are some signs that the liberal arts colleges are finally being aroused; this is evidenced by their frequent anguished cries over the deficiencies of the public schools and by the eloquent pleas made by many college presidents for the restoration of content in the secondary schools. One university is even spending several hundred thousand dollars to "study the liberal arts needs of the high schools." But, alas, for the discrepancy between good intentions and common sense—the man chosen to conduct the survey is one of the university's educationists who has stated publicly that he thinks the liberal arts in high school are only for the minority! On one campus, at least (that of the University of Illinois), a small group of scholars led by Professors Arthur Bestor, Harry Fuller, and Stewart Cairns, are battling valiantly in behalf of educational standards in the schools. I have mentioned before in these pages Professor Bestor's suggestion to the American Historical Association that it sponsor a commission drawn from the scholarly societies which would be charged with studying the school problem and recommending reforms. At the time I write this proposal seems to be in abeyance and one may be skeptical that anything will come of it; the vigor that produced educational pragmatism seems to have gone out of American academic circles, at least among those who might be expected to launch a counterrevolution. The liberal arts people were complacent at the birth of the Education monster and they have allowed it to develop unchecked over the years. I suppose that ultimately they will have to be the instrumentality through which the schools are reformed but it often seems that they have a distaste for the task and will only undertake it through public pressure.

Many persons would like to see a vigorous lay movement in behalf of better schools, and some thought such a movement was being launched when the National Citizens Commission for the Public Schools was organized a few years ago, with distinguished patronage and the financial aid of the large foundations. I think many such persons became quickly disillusioned for the early promotional literature of the Commission sounded all too often like Frank Sullivan's Mr. Arbuthnot, the cliché expert, at large in education. Those disturbed about school conditions felt that the public schools needed something more invigorating than slogans, and brochures printed on coated stock in which Truman and Eisenhower and the chairman of the board of the Standard Oil Company of New Jersey assured them that they think education is a good thing.

I regret to say that the subsequent record of the NCCPS shows it to be primarily a public-relations group with the typical approach of such a group: get as many people together as possible; assume that their collective intelligence is roughly that of a twelve-year-old; generate lots of vague good will; above all, deal in generalities and thus avoid offending anybody. The Commission has certainly been successful in getting people together for it has helped to organize hundreds of citizens groups, but it has not shown that all this activity has much to do with genuine concern for the quality of public education; although it is for "better schools" it has steadfastly refused to define what is meant by the term. As a consequence, its literature and the literature of the groups it has helped to launch, is long on eloquent pleas for better buildings and salaries (who is against them?) but short on direct and honest consideration of the purposes of schools. It is easy to believe that the Commission is in spirit the lay arm of the National Education Association, designed to sell the *status quo*. As a matter of fact, the original suggestion for the Commission came from the Educational Policies Commission of the NEA, and the present advisory panel of six persons has a preponderance of orthodox educators numbering four, including our old friend Willard Goslin. Despite the undoubted good intentions of many persons connected with it the National Citizens Commission for the Public Schools must be counted a very frail reed to lean on in the battle for better schools.

What would probably be of some help at this particular point is the formation of a small commission—academic, or part academic and part lay—which would undertake a serious study of the schools. Such a commission ought to exclude any of that pompous breed which makes a profession of serving on commissions for window dressing and it ought to exclude orthodox educators who are already on record, and voluminously, as to what they think schools are doing and what they think they ought to be doing. I think such a commission should be frankly "slanted" in that its membership should be expected to believe in *education*, not training or adjustment, as a worthy ideal for all in a democracy. Its function would be to examine the present accomplishment of the schools in the light of this ideal of genuine education and where there is a discrepancy between the ideal and the accomplishment, recommend corrective measures. Anybody who knows anything about the American educational scene can think of outstanding college presidents and professors who would make excellent members of such a commission; I can think also of several laymen with good qualifications, and even a handful of educationists who comprise a little backwater of intellectual distinction in a profession not notably distinguished in this direction.

There are various reasons why such a commission is a remote possibility. Chief among them is that the educationists have such a rigid control over public education that the work and report of such a commission would be drowned in a sea of criticism. If it exposed the real state of affairs in public education the professionals would do exactly what they have done in the case of parental committees which have criticized schools: the whole, gigantic, well-oiled machinery would go into action; the educational combine of professors of education, affiliated educational associations, and their numerous journals, would conduct a unanimous assault which would undoubtedly include the reiterated charge that the members of the commission were unfriendly to public schools. A second reason why such a commission is likely to remain in the dream state is directly related to the first reason: dissidents from the majority point of view, unless they happen to possess that fairly rare quality, moral courage, are cautious about sticking their necks out. Those who exercise this caution sometimes mistake it for "the spirit of cooperation" but fail to see that the cooperation is all on one side, theirs. Moral courage on the part of college presidents just now would have a wonderfully stimulating effect; if all of them who complain privately about the deficiencies of the schools were to unite in public complaint we might be roused out of our complacency. (A notable exception to presidential caution is Harold W. Dodds of Princeton, who, as I pointed out earlier in these pages, has spoken out in forthright fashion.)

While we are waiting for organized salvation it seems to me there are certain things parents and laymen can do on the plane of individual action. The first thing they can do—and this is axiomatic—is to inform themselves as to what is going on. This may be a somewhat dreary business for it will involve the reading of much current educational philosophy and theory, the prose style of which is apt to make the reader feel like a man stalking a bird across wet cement, to borrow a phrase of James Thurber's. The first thing parents must do is to understand the deep-seated bias of modern education which reflects the general philosophical bias of the last one hundred, and more, years, a bias involving the repudiation of ultimate truths in favor of pragmatic testing, the perversion of science into idolatry of the scientific method, the dethroning of man as individual in favor of sociological man. From this philosophical viewpoint spring many of the practices which are revolutionizing our schools. Under its aegis we are abandoning standards and refusing to acknowledge that any body of knowledge is appropriate for all men or that some subjects are intrinsically more important than others; in the name of science we are pretending to fit human beings into fixed and rigid categories of aptitude, thus perpetuating an argument made by opponents of universal education a hundred years ago, namely, that many persons are uneducable; and we are belittling man's inviolable privacy and individual responsibility and declaring that he can only find purpose as part of the collective and the group.

The teacher who ministers to your child in the third grade or the principal of his school may not think they are doing these things but if they received their professional training within the last twenty-five years the chances are ten to one that the philosophy and the practices I describe were advocated by *their* teachers. There is also the possibility, of course, that you are fortunate enough to have a principal and teachers who paid only lip service to the official dogmas while in training. As a matter of fact, if it were not for the moral courage and good common sense of thousands of teachers in maintaining an underground resistance our present plight would be considerably worse than it is. Moreover, when we consider the many teachers who have emerged without permanent intellectual damage from exposure to educational workshops, laboratories, and clinics, and summer courses in schools of education, we may venture the hope that devotion to genuine education may not be quite so readily extinguishable as its enemies think.

In your school you may have been spared, on the high school level, the blight of the core curriculum, and there may be teachers in your elementary school who think mathematics is something more than a "real life experience" which shows the pupil how to account for his lunch money. I am afraid, however, that in one form or another your school will be under *some* conviction to the educationist gospel, and this poses a pretty problem to the parent who feels strongly about standards and also wants to maintain friendly and cooperative relations with school personnel. I think it would be a mistake to attempt to establish good will at the expense of conviction—and there is always the possibility that you may be persuasive enough to make the heathen see the light. It is also true—fortunately—that many teachers are relieved when parents speak out and confirm their own doubts about the entire wisdom of modern education. If we are ever going to restore values to our school system individual parents are going to have to make themselves heard, politely but firmly, even at the risk of being accused of attacking Our Schools.

Parents ought not to be bashful, for instance, about looking over textbooks and complaining if they think they are poor. The fact that some intellectually lightweight snoopers have made complaints about textbooks (principally on the college level) does not change the circumstance that many of them *are* inferior and deserve to be complained about. Don't be intimidated by the pained cries of the professionals when a textbook is criticized; this is but the natural reaction when their untouchability is threatened. The educationists have long since established such a monopoly in this field that specialists in subject matter find it difficult to publish their textbooks unless the name of an educationist appears as coauthor; the educationist is almost never an authority in a particular subject, only an authority in how to teach it. Many of the books on the elementary school level, in trying to make their material seem attractive, succeed only in making it distasteful. Take, for example, a series called Adventures with Numbers (arithmetic to you); the individual volumes have titles such as Busy Beavers, Range Riders, Airplane Aces, and Home Run Hitters, which the authors tell us represent motifs taken from "the pupils' world" and are, they rather overoptimistically assert, "captivating to the pupil." They add an ominous, but typical, note to the teacher: "Emphasis is placed on crediting the pupil with what he does correctly without undermining his confidence when he fails to make a perfect score, or the hypothetical 100%."

Another type of book which crops up constantly in the elementary schools, especially in the field of social studies, is the textbook which propagandizes for the author's own social convictions. Harold Rugg's social studies textbooks are the perfect examples of the type; they used to have a tremendous circulation but have fallen by the wayside in recent years. I have seen a sixth-grade textbook which rings all the changes on the exploitation of the Mexican peon, first by the Spanish grandees and later by American business interests, all of which may or may not be true, or partially true, but is certainly in any case a complex subject for adult consideration, not for sixth graders who are ripe to receive and retain the *facts* about Mexico which will be of use to them later in forming adult opinions about Mexico.

Parents ought also to be wary of standards defining a good school when they are set up by educationists. Very often when parents hear that certain school systems, usually those in suburbs of large cities, are "among the finest in the country," they feel that if only they could move there, Johnny's and Mary's learning problems would be solved. If such parents will take the trouble to inquire they will find that usually the reputation of these school systems is based on the judgment of educationists and that the systems they describe as among the finest in the country are simply those which have most thoroughly and wholeheartedly adopted the greatest number of recommendations made by the professionals. Likewise when one hears a superintendent described as "one of America's ablest educators" it means only that his fellow professionals are vouching for his orthodoxy. When a school system is described as one of the finest, or a superintendent as an able educator, by a body of scholars, then the layman may have some faith in the accuracy of the judgment.

Another direction in which laymen need to exercise independent judgment is in the matter of school buildings. We seem unable in this country to strike a balance between delapidated hovels and extravagant palaces. We can all agree that school children need to be decently housed but I wonder if we couldn't be getting more classrooms and investing more money in teachers' salaries if we cut down on elaborate gymnasiums, intercommunication systems, and expensive equipment in home economics and shop rooms. (I know schools beautifully endowed in this last respect which have no libraries, or extremely meagre ones.)

Still another thing parents can do in the attempt to lessen the control of the educationists is to write to, or appear before, the education committees in the state legislature, which committees almost never hear from anybody except the educationists. If these committees were made aware of the fact that some reasonable people hold a viewpoint about certification, for instance, at variance with the official one, they might be less prone to recommend legislation that entrenches the power of the education lobby.

To the average parent and layman perhaps my plea for individual action is one he will consider no solution at all, or one he will find vague and inadequate in a time of pressing need. But has the infinite variety of our group action—our associations, committees, commissions, surveys, and studies— really advanced us very far along the road to educational reform? As a last desperate remedy perhaps we should try individual responsibility, individual initiative, individual action. Not until individual man rebels against mediocrity, spiritual illiteracy, and group subservience will our unique experiment of universal education become once again a bright hope and promise in American life.

Acknowledgments

As STATED in the Prologue, I have profited during the past few years from discussions with hundreds of persons across the country regarding matters touched upon in this book. I wish it were possible to thank each one individually but as the company is so numerous I must here content myself with collective thanks.

I am grateful to the following publishers for use of material:

To the World Book Company for permission to quote from *Fundamentals of Curriculum Development* by B. Othanel Smith, William O. Stanley, and J. Harlan Shores; and from *Patterns of Educational Philosophy* by Theodore Brameld.

To the Ronald Press Company for permission to quote from *Secondary Education for Life Adjustment of American Youth* by Harl R. Douglass.

To Harper & Brothers for permission to quote from *New Schools for a New Culture,* by Charles M. MacConnell, Ernest O. Melby, Christian O. Arndt, and Leslee J. Bishop.

To Harvard University Press for permission to quote from *Education and Liberty* by James Bryant Conant.

Once again I am grateful to my wife, Sylvea Bull Smith, for fruitful discussions and suggestions about a common interest.

Index

Index